FACTORY COST KEEPING

LINCOLN FACTORY EXECUTIVE SERVICE

A Complete Training Service in the Principles and Practice of Modern Factory Management

Editor-in-Chief

J. FRANCIS CARLE, B.S. Ed., M.A.

Educational Director, Lincoln Extension Inst. Inc. Former School Administrator in Ohio Public Schools; Former Production Engineer, Standard Aircraft Prods., Inc.

LINCOLN EXTENSION INSTITUTE, INC.

TO THE STUDENT

This textbook represents one unit of this subject. Its effectiveness depends on the proper use of the educational material and services which are supplementary to it.

It is the aim and purpose of Lincoln Extension Institute, Inc., to extend to each student only the very best of service and help which our staff is equipped to give. We invite you to write us and offer suggestions for the improvement of our instructional material and service.

LOUIS S. VOSBURGH,
President

LINCOLN
FACTORY EXECUTIVE SERVICE

FACTORY COST KEEPING

BY

COL. E. C. PECK

*Former Works Manager
Cleveland Twist Drill Co.*

Part of a Complete Systematic Training Service in
Modern Factory Management

LINCOLN EXTENSION INSTITUTE, INC.
CLEVELAND, OHIO

IN CANADA: LINCOLN INSTITUTE (CANADA) LIMITED,
TORONTO, ONT.

Copyright 1931, 1942, 1948, 1949 by the
Lincoln Extension Institute, Inc.

Printed in the United States of America
Revised Edition
Fourth Printing

THE H. W. HILL PRINTING CO., CLEVELAND, OHIO
12-52 5M

TABLE OF CONTENTS

FACTORY COST KEEPING

CHAPTER		PAGE
I	PURPOSE OF STUDYING FACTORY COST KEEPING	1

Recent Interests in Factory Cost Keeping. Limitations of This Study. Intention of This Text. Old and New Methods.

| II | VALUE OF COST SYSTEM TO A FACTORY .... | 5 |

Relation of Cost System to General Accounting. Three Reasons for Cost Systems. Its Importance to the Factory Manager. Danger of Business Without a Cost System. How the Cost System Helps the Factory. The Cost System and the Cost Department.

| III | COST SYSTEMS MUST MEET REQUIREMENTS .... | 12 |

A Cost System Must Be Built. Changed Attitude Towards Cost System. Plan Completely Before Installing. Objects of a Cost System. Requirements of a Cost System. Practical Limits of Accuracy in Costs. Accuracy in Distributing Indirect Expenses.

| IV | FUNDAMENTAL FACTORS OF COSTS .... | 16 |

Cost Factors. Three Fundamentals of Manufacturing Cost. Simple Example. First Indication of Indirect Expense. Brown Goes Into Business. Complications in Brown's Manufacturing Costs. Main Items of Indirect Expense. Further Reasons for Complexity.

| V | MATERIALS EXPENSES .... | 21 |

Determining Expense of Material. Direct and Indirect Material. Order Should Specify Unit. Materials Which Are Cut Up. Expense of Supplies.

| VI | LABOR EXPENSES .... | 27 |

Importance of Correct Labor Records. Direct Labor. Indirect Labor. Classified Labor List. Mixed Labor. Time and Piece Records Must Be Accurate. Methods in Use. Plan Must Furnish Details.

| VII | INDIRECT EXPENSE .... | 32 |

Third Fundamental. Factors of Indirect Expense. Fixed Charges. Depreciation Expense. Determining Rate of Depreciation. Variable Expense. Workmen's Compensation Insurance. Power, Heat, Light. Repairs. Factory Expenses. Percentage Method. Inaccuracy of Percentage Plan. Productive Hour Plan. Complications of Productive Hour Plan. Machine Hour Method. Arriving at Hourly Machine Rate. Machine Hour Method Modified. Value of Machine Hours. Error of Same Expense in All Departments. Estimating Previous Job, if Performed in Department A. Again Estimating Previous Job, if Performed in Department C. Departmental Expense. Applying Departmental Expense. Continuous Production System. Unit of Product.

| VIII | ACCURATE COSTS DEPEND UPON ACCURATE TIME RECORDS .... | 53 |

The Need for Accurate Original Cost Records. Recognition of the Value of Time. Relation Between Time and Cost Accounting. Time Should Be Controlled as Carefully as Materials. Workmen Are Not Trained Accountants. Time Records Essential in All Wage Payment Methods. Payroll Time and Job Time. Control of Time. Attendance Recorders. The Time Clerk. Job Cost Cards. Information on Job Cards. Job Cost Recorders.

TABLE OF CONTENTS

FACTORY COST KEEPING

CHAPTER   **PAGE**

IX   COLLECTING COSTS WITH THE AID OF MACHINES 71
Use of Machines in Offices. Electric Punched Card Accounting Machine Method. The Punched Card. The Job Card. The Continuous Job Card. The Daily Reporting Card. Punching of Perforations. The Electric End Printing Reproducing Punch. The Electric Card Punching Machine. Electric Punched Hole Verifier. The Electric Punched Card Sorting Machine. Electric Punched Card Accounting Machine. Value of Electric Punched Card Accounting Machines. Scope of Use of Electric Accounting Machine Systems. Reports Developed by Tabulating Machine Methods. Timekeeping and Payroll. Three Plans of Cost Department Routine. Advantages of Daily Reporting Plan. Time Saved in Using Tabulating Machines. Comparison with Hand Sorting and Hand Posting.

X   PAYROLL AND LABOR ACCOUNTING 102
Definition and Objectives. Labor Accounting.

XI   ADMINISTRATIVE AND SELLING EXPENSE 109
Relation Between Manufacturing and Other Expenses. Proper Application of Expense. "Cost to Manufacture." Keep Factory Cost Separate. "Cost to Distribute." Charging Interest on Investment. Relation of Interest to "Profit and Loss." Proper Charge of Interest.

XII   ANALYZING EXISTING COST SYSTEM 118
Steps in Making Analysis. Methods in Use. Frills in System. Head of Department. Questions Answered by Analysis.

XIII   FACTORY COST ACCOUNTANT 123
Personal Qualifications. Knowledge and Experience. Personal Accuracy. Tact and Diplomacy. Value Measured by Results.

XIV   COST CONTROL AND THE FACTORY EXECUTIVE 127
Where can costs be controlled? What kind of a man does it take? The Factory Executive's Cost Reports. Making Cost Control Worthwhile to the Factory Executive.

BIBLIOGRAPHY 137

INDEX 139

FACTORY COST KEEPING

"Controlling costs is a management's job that never ends."

Chapter One

PURPOSE OF STUDYING FACTORY COST KEEPING

Recent Interests in Factory Cost Keeping

1. The last ten years have shown an unusual interest in the costs of manufacturing operations. Administration executives have needed accurate cost data more than ever before in order to control the expenses of factory operation. The small difference of a fraction of a cent in the cost of each unit of several products, when taken over a year's production, has meant profit or loss for many companies. The Federal Income Tax has forced a more detailed and more accurate cost keeping system than was necessary some time ago.

The World War also had its influence by giving additional impetus to mass production, which in turn necessitated more standardization of products, automatic tools, etc. Competition became keener as quantity production increased. Manufacturers worked on a closer margin of profit per unit of production and depended on increased numbers of units to make up the reduction in unit profit. These things have resulted in a greatly increased appreciation of the importance of detailed knowledge of the costs of manufacturing, and in order to obtain such knowledge, the importance of, and necessity for accurate Cost Systems. Manufacturers' Associations, Accountants' Associations and other trade organizations are cooperating to improve the Cost Keeping of many manufacturing companies.

Limitations of This Study

2. The field of Factory Cost Keeping has become a highly specialized factor in industrial plants. Expert Cost Accountants and Industrial Engineers have set up certain cost systems within factories and have at times, failed in their handling of the situation or only met with partial successes in spite of their years of experience. So it is not to be expected that a student of this training course will become a cost accountant as a result of this brief study. One who has an intimate knowledge of the details of manufacturing, who knows all the needs of a factory, and becomes thoroughly familiar with all the principles of Cost Finding after further study, could in time feel competent to organize a system to meet the needs of a particular factory.

Intention of This Text

3. There is contained in these pages a helpful fund of information to every student in his effort to gain some knowledge of Factory Cost Keeping. A better understanding permits of closer cooperation; an increased knowledge of the problems and the efforts being made to solve them, will surely stir up a sympathy that before was perhaps an indifference or a disgust. It is the intention of this text to familiarize the student with the objects, requirements and methods in use

Factory Cost Keeping

in Factory Cost Keeping Systems. As he moves up into executive positions of more responsibility, the cost figures pertaining to his department will be more intelligible and more useful. Finally he may reach a position where he has the opportunity to analyze all the functions of the Cost System where he is employed and determine if the Cost System is fulfilling its mission or what changes should be made to increase its efficiency. The text is necessarily somewhat general in its treatment and the student must remember that the details are dependent upon the character of the manufacturing business.

Old and New Methods

4. The manufacturer of former years grew so gradually in business that he was content to figure costs in a yearly manner and take his chance on the profit. The taxes, insurance, up-keep, and depreciation for the year would be divided by twelve and charged monthly. The office and selling expense plus the labor was computed monthly. The total material used each month would be charged against the product and the grand total of all the monthly expenses divided by the number of units of product made each month would be the total cost of each unit of product. Costs so derived are called "Historical" Costs.

The manufacturer of the present time separates manufacturing costs from administrative and sales costs in order that he may analyze them more carefully and control the items of great expense. The maximum period over which the costs extend before being figured and reported is a month, and in many cases semi-monthly costs are obtained. The tendency is towards even shorter periods of time. Some Factory Cost Systems are so set up that Daily Time Cards are used where no Planning Department precludes their use. This gives a certain amount of daily control over the In Process Inventory. Where the information is held out in the shop for a week or two, the Factory Manager is not aware of all the costs in his plant and considerable mischief is done before he knows exactly where he stands. Daily Costs inform him of the accumulative costs of material and labor on the jobs going through the plant. If emergencies arise, he is enabled to proceed intelligently because he is in possession of the cost figures up to 24 hours before. Costs derived in this manner are today called "Standard" or predetermined costs. The difference between historical and standard costs is very apparent. Historical costs are those which are based upon past figures and derived *after* the product has been completed. Standard costs are based upon past figures but are derived *before* the product has been completed. Standard costs are derived prior to manufacturing from engineered standards for material, labor, and factory burden. Standard costs are usually composed of productive labor, shop expense and material consumed.

Chapter Two

VALUE OF COST SYSTEM TO A FACTORY

Relation of Cost System to General Accounting

1. In order that the executive departments of a manufacturing concern may operate intelligently, they must have at their disposal certain financial facts relative to the business. These facts are furnished, in the modern organization, by the Accounting Department. The information required by the manufacturing department is, for the most part, furnished by the Cost System. The Cost System should preferably be operated in a co-operative arrangement with the general accounting plan. Of course the information as to wages earned and material used must be obtained from the manufacturing department, but all of this information must be correlated, or "tied in," with the general financial records, since all expenditures contracted for the manufacturing department must be paid and accounted for by the Accounting Department.

Three Reasons for Cost Systems

2. (a) The first and most obvious reason why every manufacturing industry should have a Cost System is for the determination of the production costs. The determination of production costs is immensely important and well justifies the installation of a Cost System. With it, price-making can be safe and intelligent. Without it, the conduct of the sales department would be unsafe.

(b) The second reason is that the analysis of costs, operation by operation, to be secured from an efficient Cost System, supplies the Factory Manager with invaluable data from which to work in reducing costs. If it is decided to start a campaign to increase the efficiency of the factory force and to eliminate the inefficient men, then the individual records of the men will be secured from the cost records. Excessive costs are discovered and forced into notice, as are also wasteful leaks or bad conditions which make costs higher than they should be, and which, when removed, result directly in decreased costs. **An adequate** cost system also indicates fluctuations in production costs and shows just where these variations take place.

(c) Increased efficiency is the third reason why every industry should have a Cost System. The Cost System in its operations indicates the consumption of material, the time and cost of every labor operation, and the performance of every separate machine. This enables the Factory Manager to judge whether men and machinery are measuring up to the proper standards of efficiency, and whether adequate results are being obtained from material. It is obvious that the highest efficiency is not possible unless any failures to attain this standard are known. Such failures the Cost System will reveal. When efficiency failures are suspected or known to exist, the cost records will show just what and where these failures are.

Its Importance to the Factory Manager

3. The greatest use of the Factory Cost System will be to the Factory Manager, as the information it furnishes is of vital importance to him in operating the factory. It furnishes him with the tabulated history of each operation, so that by careful analysis he will be able to locate and correct the inefficient ones. It will enable him to pick out the most efficient men, machines and methods, and use them as standards to which to bring up the rest. It presents the details of the unprofitable labor to him in such a manner that he is enabled to find out definitely if it is required, and, if not, to eliminate it. It gives him the details of the heat, light and power expense, that they may be analyzed for useless expense or waste. He is enabled through the information it furnishes to know if money is wasted on repairs or shop supplies and if full value is obtained from special tools and fixtures. It furnishes the information which gives the control of production by informing the Factory Manager the output of the machines, and the idle hours caused from stoppage or failure of material to reach them.

Danger of Business Without a Cost System

4. Every industry should know exactly what it costs to manufacture the products and all healthy ones do. There are still some industries today, however, that do not know their costs and make no pretense of finding them. There are others who think they know and are fooling themselves with a book profit which never materializes. It must be plain to any thinking man that a business without a good Cost System is in as much danger as a ship without a rudder. The rudder guides the ship in its proper course when properly operated by a competent pilot. The Cost System guides the business in its proper financial course when managed by a competent man. A manufacturer who insists on doing business without knowing his costs is inviting disaster just as much as though he sold at unknown prices, because he is guessing. As soon as competition becomes keen enough, such a manufacturing business will be forced to the wall.

How the Cost System Helps the Factory

5. It points out the profitable articles of manufacture so that these may be pushed, and the sales increased. It points out those articles

Factory Cost Keeping

which should have their selling price raised or their manufacturing costs reduced. When times are dull and competition is keen, it tells exactly how far a price can be reduced without actual loss. The manufacturer who does not know his costs may be selling at a loss when competing with another manufacturer. Those who know their costs can reduce prices safely so there is still a margin of profit. These points of advantage which are obtained with the aid of the Factory Cost System are very vital to any business and well worth the outlay of money and time expended wisely on such a system.

The Cost System and the Cost Department

6. In setting up a Cost System the Cost Department has one purpose in view; that being to handle accurately the moneys with which a business concern operates. This is true whether the plant employs 10,000 men or 10 men. The fundamentals are the same. Some cost systems are complicated, while others are simple and very easily understood, but the fundamentals still remain the same. The few differences exist only in the details and ways in which these fundamentals are adapted to the peculiarities or differences of the business carried on. This thought may find repetition later in this Text, however, it should be kept firmly in mind since this Text presents the basic fundamentals which the student is expected to adapt to his own work.

The factory executive will be held responsible to a great degree for determining where and how costs may be reduced or kept down. His job will not deal with finding different ways to fit cost keeping fundamentals even though he must know all the fundamentals well. The job of adaptation of cost keeping and finding, however, is not relegated to the factory executive, but to the Cost Department. The work of the Cost Department in carrying out its purposes (page 5, paragraph 2) is often divided into these functions or operations:

1. Gathering all cost information from every department in the plant and its offices.

The work involved in gathering the cost information is a matter of providing blank forms competent enough to require and hold necessary cost information—then making certain these forms are handed in or picked up regularly, expediently, and on time.

2. Distributing direct labor costs and material costs.

The operation above is strictly a cost department function which involves applying cost keeping fundamentals to the peculiarities of the business. It involves charging all the labor and materials which have gone into the actual making of the product.

FACTORY COST KEEPING

3. Calculation of all other costs involved in fabricating the final product.

The range of costs taken in by this function include such items as insurance, rent, and labor from non-productive personnel which includes millwright, maintenance men, and inspectors. These costs include materials and supplies which *do not* enter directly into the final product, process or operation, but which make up a considerable part of the cost of producing an article. Expenditures for lubricating fluids, tools, dies, etc. are included in such costs.

The gathering and calculating of such material costs whether direct or indirect is specifically a Cost Department controlled function. It is here that cost control efficiency can be started. The factory executive who is familiar with the foregoing facts regarding the specific activities of the Cost Department has "his foot in the door" to cost economy since it is the least understood activity of the Cost Department. Most detailed information and practice in dealing with material expenses and costs will be taken up in the chapters that follow.

Chapter Three

COST SYSTEMS MUST MEET REQUIREMENTS

A Cost System Must Be Built

1. The proper Cost System for one line of manufacture may be entirely unsuited to another as regards the details of operation. The Cost System is the most intricate of all accounting systems and must be carefully designed to suit the exact requirements of each individual business. A good Cost System cannot be purchased ready made, nor can it always be installed without some changes in the methods of doing business. Usually, the more systematically the factory has been operated, the easier it is to design, install, and operate a Cost System.

Changed Attitude Towards Cost System

2. At first cost systems were planned, built and operated by an accountant who had little knowledge of manufacturing, and whose sole aim was to get an array of figures that in his judgment represented costs and balanced out properly at the end of the month or year, according to the period adopted. The needs of the Factory Manager were not always understood; he was expected to produce with the greatest economy, by certain inherent ability or skilled work, but no part of the cost finding records were collected or tabulated for his special guidance. In many industries today, the Factory Costing Staff reports to the Factory Manager, and collects for the Factory Manager the cost records which form his control of costs or the economy of production.

Plan Completely Before Installing

3. The general plan and the objects sought must be entirely worked out before a start is made, then each step thoroughly inaugurated and proved before attempting the next. It now seems pertinent to ask, "What is a Cost System for and who is to use it?"

Objects of a Cost System

4. Figure 1 represents graphically what a Cost System is for and who obtains the benefits of it. The primary object of a Cost System is to find the detailed cost of production. It also furnishes the necessary information to make up the payroll and check it. It furnishes the detailed information as regards the productive hours of both men and machines in such a manner that a constant check is obtained on the economy of production. It furnishes information which helps to make up a statement of assets and liabilities and a profit and loss statement. It facilitates business by showing definitely at what price and how much business can be taken.

Requirements of a Cost System

5. The most important requirement of a Cost System is accuracy, because it must be relied upon at all times to furnish information necessary to guide the business. If it is

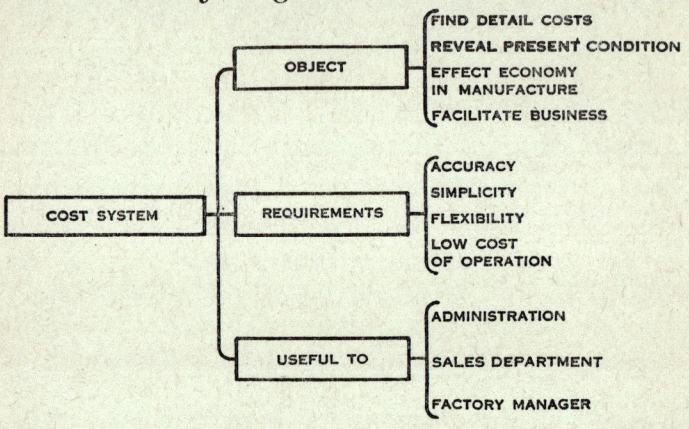

```
                              ┌─ FIND DETAIL COSTS
                   ┌─ OBJECT ─┤─ REVEAL PRESENT CONDITION
                   │          │─ EFFECT ECONOMY IN MANUFACTURE
                   │          └─ FACILITATE BUSINESS
                   │
                   │                ┌─ ACCURACY
COST SYSTEM ───────┼─ REQUIREMENTS ─┤─ SIMPLICITY
                   │                │─ FLEXIBILITY
                   │                └─ LOW COST OF OPERATION
                   │
                   │             ┌─ ADMINISTRATION
                   └─ USEFUL TO ─┤─ SALES DEPARTMENT
                                 └─ FACTORY MANAGER
```

FIGURE 1. *Graphic Outline of a typical Factory Cost System.*

not accurate, losses may be caused by overpricing some products, driving profitable business to competitors, and by underpricing other products thereby inviting direct losses. It must be as simple as possible, both to avoid error and unnecessary records and the time spent to collect them. It must be flexible enough to lend itself to changes of manufacture without disrupting the system. It must not be so complicated or cumbersome that the cost of operation is out of proportion to the value of the information obtained.

Practical Limits of Accuracy in Costs

6. This paragraph must not be taken to detract from the statement that accuracy is one of the requirements of a Cost System. There is a limit to which it is profitable to carry the analysis of factory costs, particularly those pertaining to Indirect Expense. The degree of accuracy that is worth while should be carefully determined to avoid the expense of getting figures that in the end would not be worth what they cost to obtain. Time may be wasted carrying out amounts to the fourth or fifth significant figure, when no figure beyond the second or third is assuredly correct, and if it were it would make no difference as to the analysis or the deduction made from the analysis. The distribution of the Indirect Expense cannot be exact; therefore it must be arbitrary but should at the same time be logical. For bookkeeping, the total as to any one item, such as Power Expense, must be correct, but the distribution cannot be, and for analysis need not be *exactly* accurate.

Accuracy in Distributing Indirect Expenses

7. Indirect expenses should be charged as nearly as possible to the factory divisions, or to the products benefited. One should not hesitate to divide the indirect expense into several parts relating to definite processes or functions, whenever it will assist in securing greater accuracy.

Chapter Four

FUNDAMENTAL FACTORS OF COSTS

Cost Factors

1. There are three fundamental elements which enter into the cost of a manufactured product. These are: Material, Wages, and Indirect Manufacturing Expenses. In order to determine the "Total Cost" we must include the Selling and Administrative Expenses. The difference between this Total Cost and the Selling Price is Profit or Loss.

Three Fundamentals of Manufacturing Cost

2. The three fundamental factors which enter into the expense of making any article or form the basis of any Cost System are graphically shown in Figure 2. A system

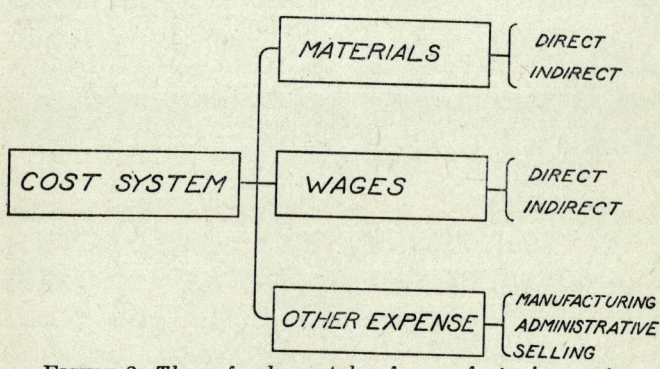

FIGURE 2. *Three fundamentals of manufacturing costs.*

which will correctly find the cost of material and labor on any article, together with its

Factory Cost Keeping

proportionate share of indirect expense, is a correct cost finding system. The one which will do this for the least expenditure of time and money without sacrificing necessary detail is the best one. Cost finding in its simplest form is illustrated in the following paragraphs.

Simple Example

3. John Smith hires Tom Brown to make boxes at 13 cts. each. Smith to furnish lumber and nails delivered to Brown, who in turn delivers finished boxes at Smith's shipping platform at above price. Smith has delivered to Brown 20,000 feet of lumber and 400 lbs. of nails which cost $510.00. Brown delivers to freight house, 950 boxes for which he receives $123.50. It is very simple to figure that these boxes cost Smith $510.00 for material and $123.50 for labor, or a total of $633.50 for the 950 boxes, which is $00.6668 each. In this example it is assumed that there was no lumber nor nails left. If there had been, these might be used on the next lot of boxes, or sold or included in the cost of the 950 and left in storage. It is plain that our simple method of figuring would be complicated somewhat by having any material left over.

First Indication of Indirect Expense

4. Suppose that Brown had been working by the day and the boxes were finished in the middle of the afternoon. There being no more work for Brown that afternoon, he fixed up his tools the balance of the day. This would also complicate the finding of the exact cost of each box. Smith is not concerned in Brown's tools, and only pays for making boxes. Finally, however, Smith realizes that Brown can make more boxes with good tools than with poor tools, and allows this time to be charged. This time for fixing tools represents the simplest form of indirect expense. It is easily divided up into the cost of each box and the cost so figured is correct.

Brown Goes Into Business

5. For purposes of further illustration let us suppose Brown has made money on the boxes and decides to go into business on a larger scale. He buys some land, erects a shop and store house for lumber and boxes. He installs a motor driven saw and employs several men and women to make the boxes for him.

Complications in Brown's Manufacturing Costs

6. Brown's problem of finding the cost of each box is now more complicated because the taxes, insurance, up-keep and a reasonable allowance for depreciation enter into the cost of manufacture. The cost of electric current used must also be included in the cost of manufacture. Lumber will have to be unloaded and piled up. This must be paid for and is a part of the cost, as well as the cutting up and nailing into boxes. Of course at the end of a month the total of all the above expenses plus those of office and selling expenses if there were any, divided by the number of boxes made, would be the total cost of each box for the month. After several months' experience he would be able to arrive at a standard cost for that particular type of box.

Main Items of Indirect Expense

7. The **taxes** mentioned in the previous paragraph are the taxes which would have to be paid on the real estate, buildings, machinery and value of any lumber in storage. The **insurance** would be that on buildings, machinery and material. The up-keep would be the money spent on keeping the buildings, machinery and tools in good working condition. The **depreciation** is an amount set aside out of the earnings each year, to replace the building and the equipment when they are worn out, obsolete, or so inefficient that they cannot be operated with profit. To illustrate: A building or machine with good care may be estimated to last fifteen years. Then, to provide for the cost of replacement at the end of 15 years, 1/15 of this cost is charged against each year's business as an expense and carried as a depreciation reserve, so that when

Factory Executive Service

the building or machine requires replacing at the end of this time, the expense has been provided for.

Further Reasons for Complexity

8. When, however, we realize that most industries manufacture a number of articles of different kinds and sizes, we commence to get an idea of the complexity of the cost finding problem. Some companies manufacture thousands of different items as the Goodrich Rubber Company, Akron, Ohio, which manufactures over 32,000 different articles of rubber. Some articles require very much more expensive machinery or labor than others. Some take more time in process or occupy more of the floor space or require more power and supervision. The selling and advertising expense on one article may be much greater than for another and all these items tend to make the problem more complex and harder to get correct costs.

Chapter Five
MATERIAL EXPENSES

Determining Expense of Material

1. There should be no great difficulty in outlining a system for determining the Expense of Material. The principal precaution in connection with the accounting for Material is a well-organized Stores Department, as outlined in another text of this training service entitled: "Materials and Supplies." The Stores Department should be impressed with the necessity of watching the property entrusted in its care with the same vigilance that the cashier exercises over the cash which has been entrusted to him. No material should be issued from the Stores without the proper record being made of such issue.

Direct and Indirect Material

2. In Figure 2, the Expense of Material as one of the three fundamentals in a Cost System, is divided into two classes which are called Direct Material and Indirect Material. Direct Material includes the actual raw material, semi-finished, and finished material of which the product is made. Indirect Material includes those materials which are utilized in manufacturing the product, but of which only a small amount is used in any one unit of the product. The quantity for a day's run may be requisitioned in a bulk lot and from this bulk lot a little of the material is used in fabricating each unit of the product. The amount required is so small that it is not economical to keep a separate record of that item of material for each unit of the product. The better plan is to take the several items of indirect material used in a number of units of the same piece of product and secure a total amount of all indirect material used in making those units. The total, in such case, divided by the number of units manufactured, would give a fair average charge for the indirect material per unit of that product.

Order Should Specify Unit

3. The unit of measure for material may be pounds, inches, surface measure, volume or count, and the order to manufacture should specify the unit measure preferably before presentation to a store room. The reason for this is that it forms a guide to the storekeeper to avoid possible errors in his specified quantity. All orders should indicate the number of units of measure for the entire order when material is issued, unless the plan of the Cost System provides for material tickets, sent direct to the Cost Department from the store room with number of shop order or job order. Tables may be made up showing the amounts of material in the most convenient multiple units of measure and in some cases even priced for ready extension of the cost sheet.

Cost sheets are made up for each order after it has been decided to manufacture a given amount of the product. The Production order

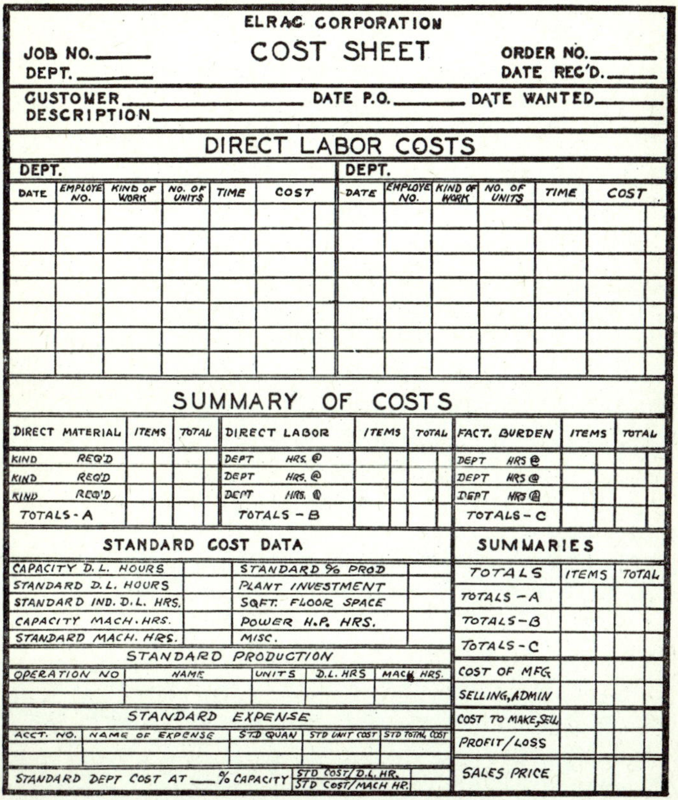
ELRAC CORPORATION

COST SHEET

JOB NO. ______ DEPT. ______ ORDER NO. ______ DATE REC'D. ______

CUSTOMER ______ DATE P.O. ______ DATE WANTED ______

DESCRIPTION ______

DIRECT LABOR COSTS

DEPT.						DEPT.					
DATE	EMPLOYE NO.	KIND OF WORK	NO. OF UNITS	TIME	COST	DATE	EMPLOYE NO.	KIND OF WORK	NO. OF UNITS	TIME	COST

SUMMARY OF COSTS

DIRECT MATERIAL	ITEMS	TOTAL	DIRECT LABOR	ITEMS	TOTAL	FACT. BURDEN	ITEMS	TOTAL
KIND REQ'D			DEPT HRS. @			DEPT HRS @		
KIND REQ'D			DEPT HRS. @			DEPT HRS @		
KIND REQ'D			DEPT HRS. @			DEPT HRS @		
TOTALS - A			TOTALS - B			TOTALS - C		

STANDARD COST DATA

CAPACITY D.L. HOURS		STANDARD % PROD	
STANDARD D.L. HOURS		PLANT INVESTMENT	
STANDARD IND. D.L. HRS.		SQ.FT. FLOOR SPACE	
CAPACITY MACH. HRS.		POWER H.P. HRS.	
STANDARD MACH. HRS.		MISC.	

STANDARD PRODUCTION

OPERATION NO	NAME	UNITS	D.L. HRS	MACH. HRS.

STANDARD EXPENSE

ACCT. NO.	NAME OF EXPENSE	STD QUAN	STD UNIT COST	STD TOTAL COST

STANDARD DEPT COST AT ___ % CAPACITY — STD COST/D.L. HR. — STD COST/MACH HR.

SUMMARIES

TOTALS	ITEMS	TOTAL
TOTALS - A		
TOTALS - B		
TOTALS - C		
COST OF MFG.		
SELLING, ADMIN		
COST TO MAKE, SELL		
PROFIT/LOSS		
SALES PRICE		

FIGURE 2a. *A typical Cost Sheet.*

is issued to the Manufacturing department, and at the same time the Cost department is ordered to begin collecting the costs of the work. These costs are accumulated on what is known as a "cost sheet." In this cost sheet are recorded the actual costs of direct labor, direct material and overhead. The manufacturing costs are thus brought together on one form. A unit cost can easily be obtained from the Cost Sheet by dividing the number of units produced into the total cost. Figure 2a is one example of a Cost Sheet.

Forms of cost sheets vary according to the needs of the particular business, as do all factory cost keeping record forms. The form shown in Figure 2a has been composed mainly to show the main subdivisions of a production cost sheet. The small section on Standard Cost Data does not necessarily or always appear on a production cost sheet, but is ordinarily on a single sheet by itself. It is included here to convey the means by which such data is recorded or posted.

Materials Which Are Cut Up

4.   When the manufacturing operations require that the material be cut up for the order before leaving the store room there is always some waste or scrap which must be considered in the cost of materials. If the waste or scrap were not considered, there would be a discrepancy sooner or later between the actual material in stock and what is supposed to be there as indicated by the inventory records. There are two common

FACTORY COST KEEPING

methods of taking care of this discrepancy. One method is to price the material on the order a fraction higher than the cost of it as laid down in the store room. By careful judgment in setting this excess price, based on past performances, the credit to the Material Account will absorb the waste or loss through scrap. In this way the usual discrepancy between the gross material in inventory records and the net material issued to orders is made up by charging a small fraction of the cost to the various orders. It is recognized that some place in the course of any period, as over thirty days, this discrepancy between the actual stock and inventory record creeps in. By distributing the slight increase in price over a number of orders, no one would feel the added price but there would be a close balance between actual stock and inventory records.

4a. The other method of handling this discrepancy is to note the exact amount of scrap or waste which results from cutting the stock for the Order. This amount of scrap is noted on the Order. The Order is charged with the actual material and the Scrap Account is charged with the waste. The total of the Material Account is thus decreased by an amount equal to the amount charged to the Scrap Account. A report of this monthly waste is of assistance to the Factory Manager in enabling him to keep this item at a low figure.

On the other hand, the scrap may be sold as salvage material or used for other purposes. The value realized from the scrap is credited to the Scrap Account. This method enables all the Material to be accounted for, and, if desired, the amount that either the Material Account or Scrap Account is out of balance may be absorbed by the General Factory Expense.

Expense of Supplies

5. The expense of supplies includes the expenses of all articles which are consumed in the manufacturing operations which are not in themselves materials that become a part of the product and therefore cannot be charged to the product as direct or indirect material. The Supplies Account includes such items as sandpaper, emery paper, lubricating oil, wiping cloths, and small perishable tools such as files, drills, etc. Supplies are issued from the Stores Department on requisitions usually originated by the department in which the articles are used. Such items should be charged to the departments as monthly supplies and considered a part of the Departmental Expenses.

Chapter Six

LABOR EXPENSES

Importance of Correct Labor Records

1. The importance of the second fundamental, the Expense of Labor, is not usually appreciated. At least this may be assumed in a factory where a large number of workmen are allowed to make out their own time. For instance, if there were one thousand 60 cent men, each of whom made an error of 15 minutes a day (a very small average), the amount of money represented by this error in the costs would be $150.00 per day.

Direct Labor

2. The Labor of a factory, like Material, is of two distinct kinds—Direct and Indirect. Direct Labor is that which can be shown to have been performed on one job or order. The total wages for this labor can all be divided between the number of pieces on the job or order, so that each piece can be charged with its exact share of the labor put upon it. The cost data is so collected that the Direct Wages of each piece can be distributed in detail for each operation performed. Direct Wages are charged to the cost of the article as soon as the labor has been completed.

Indirect Labor

3. The second kind of labor is that which cannot be directly charged to individual orders, jobs or pieces with a fair degree of accuracy. This kind of labor is often called Indirect Labor but is sometimes miscalled Non-Productive Labor. We prefer to use the term Indirect Labor because there really is no labor that produces nothing. Both Direct and Indirect Labor are needed. Indirect Labor represents such labor as cleaning the factory, trucking, clerical work, storekeeping, inspection, and supervision. It is easily seen that each order or article could not be charged directly with its share of the Indirect Wages, and yet it is essential to manufacturing. All the items of Indirect Wages are determined from a payroll distribution. A popular method is to charge the Indirect Wages to the department in which such labor is performed. The other method is to collect all the Indirect Wages with other Indirect Expense items into the General Factory Expense and pro rate the total of the General Factory Expense back to the different departments of the factory. The disadvantage of this latter method is that the Indirect Labor of each department does not generally appear by itself and consequently is harder to control.

Classified Labor List

4. The superintendent, foremen, time clerks, and cost clerks have a classified list of the Direct and Indirect Labor for each department. Some organizations further distinguish between the two classes of labor by having different colored Attendance Record Cards on which the time records are printed. When arranged in the card racks, anyone can see at a glance those who are on the regular Direct Labor Payroll and the employees who are classified within the Indirect Labor Payroll.

Mixed Labor

5. Where all of the work performed is paid for by the piece, hundred or other number of units, it is a comparatively simple matter to obtain the Direct Wages. Where both piece work or bonus system and day work is in use, it is more difficult to obtain the Direct Wages, especially if some workmen work a part of the time on day work basis and part of the time on piece work basis. In factories where workmen change from one basis of wage payment to another, as piece rate to day rate, they are prone to reduce the piece work hours and increase the day work hours as a means of increasing their wages. After they are "rung in" on the day work, they sometimes finish the piece work jobs which they had reported as completed. Or they start piece work jobs while still "rung in" on day work basis. The closest supervision is necessary at times to detect and prevent this from being done. It is not only dishonest but it causes the cost figures to be inaccurate and unreliable.

Time and Piece Records Must Be Accurate

6. It is obvious that costs obtained this way are incorrect and are not a reliable basis for large estimates. The Labor Record should be as accurate as possible to secure without making the cost of collecting it out of proportion to the results obtained.

Methods in Use

7. There are many methods of getting time records, from guessing, to systems of time recorders arranged to print the time of starting a piece of work, and the time of finishing. The elapsed time or actual time on the work is the difference between the two time imprints. If the Cost System is planned to fit one of these clock-controlled period-printing methods, labor expenses are usually found accurately and satisfactorily. There are a number of these time recorder systems on the market which have proven economical and reliable. In Chapter 8: *Accurate Costs Depend Upon Accurate Time Records,* the time recorder systems are explained in detail.

FACTORY COST KEEPING

Plan Must Furnish Details

8. The Cost System must be so planned that the information furnished the Cost Department contains the following essential details pertaining to the wages of labor. These may be reported on the Job Tickets, Shop Orders or special form of ticket provided for the purpose.

(1) The time worked on any job or order by each workman and the number of pieces accepted and the necessary information to enable the payroll department to make up the payroll.

(2) A means to check the payroll against the actual production, so as to avoid paying for the same work twice, or paying for piece work and day work both on the same operation.

(3) A further check to see that the total wages—Direct and Indirect, charged to the product, agrees with the amount expended by the payroll department in the form of wages for work done by manufacturing departments. The wages paid for maintenance work come within a separate classification.

(4) A means of collecting for each job the number of machine hours worked either individually or by groups, according to the plan in use. (If the machine hour plan is used.)

(5) A method of notifying the Cost Department how many machines the operator is running; also if his day work card contains the full time of operation on any piece of work performed on a day work basis, in one machine, when operating two or more machines.

(6) The immediate notification of any change in method which will affect the rates paid for the labor.

(7) A means to collect all of the Indirect Wages by departments.

CHAPTER SEVEN

INDIRECT EXPENSE

Third Fundamental

1. The third fundamental of a Cost System, Indirect Expense, is the hardest of all to fully understand because of its many complications. Indirect Expense is composed of items that relate to the factory as a whole, to departments or to divisions, but not to factory orders. It generally is the weakest point of a poor system; and by the same test the accuracy of classifying and handling the Indirect Expenses shows the merits of a good system. The problem of accurate costing is to charge each expense to the product in which it is involved in correct amounts to the ratio of use and benefits. Some of the indirect expenses relate to the processes of production, and wherever possible these should be charged directly to the processes so that they with other expenses of processing will be charged on the product being processed. For example, depreciation relates to the normal useful life of specified equipment. Since the various processes require different kinds of equipment and the depreciation rates may differ widely as between processes, it is better to consider this item separately by processing divisions or departments, rather than to use the total depreciation as a basis and arbitrarily distribute it as a general expense.

Factors of Indirect Expense

2. The Indirect Expense of an article must include its correct proportion of (1) The Indirect Materials or Supplies, (2) The Indirect Wages, (3) The Machine Expense, (4) Taxes, Insurance, Depreciation, Up-keep of Buildings and Equipment, Light, Heat, Power and the Interest Charge on the investment. In fact the Indirect Expense must include its proportionate share of all the expense of conducting the business before it is known at what price the article can be profitably sold. These items of Indirect Expense are divided into two main classes of this expense—Fixed Charges and Variable Charges.

Fixed Charges

3. Fixed Charges comprise those items of expense which have to be paid regardless of whether the plant operates or not. They are in general beyond the control of the Factory Manager. Fixed Charges consist of the following items: Rent or its equivalent (chargeable on the basis of floor area), Taxes, Depreciation, Insurance, Interest on Investment are all chargeable on the basis of investment required to produce the product. This basis is explained as follows: An item of product which is made on an expensive machine or one which occupies a large amount of floor space, will cost more, so far as Fixed Charges per hour are concerned, than one which is made on the less expensive machine or which occupies a smaller amount of floor space and considerably more than if the part or product is made at the bench.

Depreciation Expense

4. Depreciation is one of the most important fixed charges which must be handled in a Factory Cost Department. It is the most uncertain and most perplexing to manufacturers because of the difficulties of determining the probable useful life of machinery, equipment and buildings. *Depreciation* is the decreasing or falling in value of any asset due to: (1) obsolescence; (2) inutility; and (3) wear and tear, and action of the elements. Inutility is lack of usefulness caused by cessation of demand for product. This applies to buildings and all types of manufacturing and office equipment. The purpose of carrying a Depreciation Account and charging a small amount of depreciation to each unit of the product is to protect the capital that is tied up in the assets. The credits to the Replacement Reserve keep the amount of capital invested in the asset at its original amount. Replacement Reserve should be carried in cash or sound securities.

Determining Rate of Depreciation

5. There are several different methods of computing depreciation but that method known as the "straight line" method is almost universally adopted by manufacturers in

Factory Cost Keeping

preference to other methods. When an asset goes on the company's books, an estimate is made of the expected life in years of the asset and of its scrap value at the end of those years. The original cost less the scrap value gives the amount of depreciation to be provided during the estimated life. This amount of depreciation divided by the number of years of estimated life gives the annual depreciation expense. If this is divided by 12, it gives the monthly depreciation charge. This is illustrated by taking a delivery truck for which a manufacturer pays $2500. Its estimated life is five years and scrap value at $100. Then $2500 less $100 gives $2400 depreciation amount. $2400 divided by five (years of useful life) gives $480 annual depreciation charge and $480 divided by 12 gives $40 monthly depreciation charge. This amount of $40 per month must then be charged into the cost of the products (with other charges) which the manufacturer may deliver to points of consumption or shipping. If less than this is charged into the cost of the product and credited to the Replacement Reserve, when the truck becomes worn out there will not be enough set up to replace it. On the other hand if all the depreciation is charged off in one year or at the rate of $200 per month, the customers who purchase the commodities delivered by the manufacturer the first year, would be paying the burden of depreciation while the customers purchasing the commodities the other four years would not be paying any portion of the depreciation burden. The student can see how, if the life of the truck is five years, that one-fifth of its depreciation amount should be charged each year to the cost of the product and set aside as a Replacement Reserve. Any other division would be incorrect or unfair to either the manufacturer or the customer.

Variable Expense

6. The Variable Charges consist of the following items of expense: Direct Wages, Indirect Wages, Manufacturing Supplies, Power, Workmen's Compensation Insurance, Repairs, and General Factory Expense. The amounts of these items vary with the schedule of production and with other conditions, such as weather conditions, hazards and accidents in the work, etc. Explanation has been previously given about Indirect Wages in Chapter 6: *Labor Expenses*. The student can easily see how the items of Supplies and Power vary directly with the amount of product turned out. The item of Workmen's Compensation Insurance increases as more workers are employed or as the work becomes more hazardous. The item of Repairs will vary with the conditions of the machinery, equipment and amount of work in the Department. Whenever the demand for products is great, only

Factory Cost Keeping

the very necessary repairs are made in order not to tie up production.

Workmen's Compensation Insurance

7. Premiums on Workmen's Compensation Insurance are paid to the insurance companies or State in amounts dependent upon the number of workers employed in different occupations. The greater the hazard, the larger the premium required. Where factories carry their own insurance or have elaborate safety organizations, the cost of the accident prevention and safety engineering is prorated among the departments on some fair basis such as number of employees or dangers of the work itself.

Power, Heat, Light

8. Electricity for Power may be generated in the factory power plant or purchased from a public utilities service company. In either case the Expense must be distributed on a fair basis to the departments which use power. Heat, Light, etc., may be likewise distributed on the basis of square feet of floor area occupied.

Repairs

9. Repairs are sometimes treated as a Fixed Charge, and if so, are charged to the various departments on the basis of the investment. However, repairs are b e t t e r charged, when incurred, directly to the department benefited; and sometimes charged to the tool, machine or other equipment re-repaired, if detailed analysis is desired. The following distinction should be made between "repairs" and "rebuilding": *Repairs* make the machine serviceable after parts worn or damaged have been replaced or repaired, but do not increase the useful life of the machine, and are therefore current expense. *Rebuilding* includes replacement of all weak or worn parts so that the term of usefulness is increased. This outlay is a capital investment to be included in the basis of depreciation charges.

Factory Expenses

10. This includes all Expense items which cannot be charged directly to any one department nor prorated on a fair basis without entailing too much clerical labor. The total is usually distributed to departments on the basis of the number of men in each department. Those who are to benefit by the cost figures should determine what items, as mentioned in preceding paragraphs, should be carried in the Factory Expense and what should be distributed to the individual departments and included in Departmental Rates. In general, it is desirable to charge directly to departments until a point is reached where the benefits of detailed expenses are overshadowed by the clerical expense of obtaining them. Conditions in different plants will also influence the method of distributing the charges. For example, where great quantities of raw material are used, it may be advisable to subdivide and distribute the Factory Expenses so that the raw material is charged with the expense up to the time and place where and when it is requisitioned out of Stores by the Production Department. Again in some industries it may be advisable to subdivide Factory Expense into: (a) man-hour rate; (b) machine-hour rate; (c) department-hour rate; (d) general manufacturing-hour rate.

Percentage Method

11. The Indirect Expense of manufactured products must be collected and prorated over the various products in a fair and equitable manner. A common method, used extensively, is to find the total of all the expenses, mentioned in the previous paragraphs, in dollars, and divide this sum by the total number of dollars of Direct Wages. The quotient thus obtained is the amount of dollars to be added for expense to each dollar's worth of

Direct Wages. For example, suppose the total Indirect Expense for a given month is $257,000 and that the Direct Wages for the same period is $100,000. By dividing the $257,000 by $100,000 the quotient obtained is $2.57. This figure is used as the basis for determining the amount of Indirect Expense to be carried by the manufactured article. If a certain article involved $5.00 worth of Productive Labor, its share of Indirect Expense would be, 2.57 x $5 or $13.85. The $13.85, Indirect Expense, plus $5.00, Direct Wages, plus the Direct Material, would give the Manufacturing Cost of the Product.

Inaccuracy of Percentage Plan

12. The Percentage Method will give correct results only when the business is considered as a whole unit and for equal periods of time. Its unfairness for individual costs is readily apparent when comparing the expense rate of a high-priced man with a low-priced. If the rate of expense is 100 percent, an 80 cent man's time would be charged at $1.60 per hour, while a 40 cent man's time would only be charged at 80 cents. It is easily proven that the cheaper man requires a larger share of both supervision and equipment upkeep, and yet only half as much is charged for him. Another thing, costs will be unfairly inflated in times of rapidly increasing wages before a readjustment of the rate takes place.

We do not think the Percentage Plan has anything which recommends it, except simplicity of operation.

Productive Hour Plan

13. There is, however, another plan which is attracting considerable attention that is known as the Productive Hour Plan. In this plan, the expense charges are divided by the total number of productive hours and the quotient represents the amount of money to be added to the regular cost per hour for each hour of labor performed. It makes no difference what the wages of the workman are, the addition of expense by this system is the same for each man per hour. The exponents of the average Productive Hour method assert that the Percentage basis cannot be a fair one, especially if there is any variation in products. They cite such examples as this: Suppose that workman, A, receives 80 cents an hour and works an 8 hour day at a bench, while workman, B, at 50 cents an hour works his 8 hours on a machine consuming a large amount of power and representing a considerable investment. A's earnings would be $6.40 per day and B's earnings would be $4.00. Exponents of the Productive Hour System claim the Percentage Method would not distribute the expense fairly. If the rate is 110 per cent, then A's job would carry $7.04 expense, while B's job would carry only $4.40.

The machine job should certainly carry as large a share of the expense and in many cases should carry much more than the bench job.

13a. Under the average Productive Hour System each man's job in the above case of A and B, would have the same expense which in this instance would be a much fairer distribution of the expense. If the Expense Distribution figured 80 cents per hour, the charge in each case would be 8 hours x 80 cents or $6.40 additional. Again, two employees may be operating lathes, one a 20-cent per hour apprentice and the other a journeyman at 80 cents per hour. Applying the Productive Hour Plan, with the Expense Distribution figures at 80 cents per hour and for an 8-hour day, the expense charge would be $6.40 against each job and machine. Using the Percentage Plan, if the rate of expense is 110 per cent, the apprentice's job would have but $1.76 per day added as expense, whereas the journeyman's job would have 110 per cent of $6.40 or $7.04 per day added as expense. It is obvious that this is not a fair distribution as it increases the charge against the machine that produces the better quality and quantity of work even if the machine itself is exactly a duplicate of the lathe operated by the apprentice.

Complications of Productive Hour Plan

14. This Productive Hour Plan becomes somewhat complicated in a large factory using both piece work and day work. All piece work would have to be paid for by the piece and then the Labor Expenses either reduced to hours at a certain rate per hour or else take the actual number of hours consumed in doing the work. This leaves chances for error in computation, which might affect the correctness of the Total Expense.

Machine Hour Method

15. In both the Percentage Method and Productive Hour Method, the entire machine expense is a part of the total Factory Expense and no discrimination is made between a piece of work performed on a highly specialized machine and one done at the bench or on a cheap machine. It is evidently incorrect and misleading to charge the same overhead to a man at a bench as to a man at a costly, space-using and power-using machine. The accuracy of these methods depends somewhat on balancing the averages over a long period. It seems perfectly logical to have a job done on a very high-priced special machine carry more of the Machine Expense than if the job were done on a cheaper machine. A method of doing this is finding a great deal of favor with engineers who are studying cost finding. This method divides Cost Finding into four heads, namely: Material, Labor, Machine Expense and Indirect Expense. The Machine Expense is not included in Indirect Expense but it is handled as a separate direct charge. The Indirect Expense includes: supervision, timekeeping, transportation of material around the shop, inspection, insurance, taxes, heat, light, and other items which make up the regular manufacturing expenses that have no relation whatever to the Machine Expense.

Arriving at Hourly Machine Rate

16. The Machine Hour Method of calculating Indirect Expense is based on the theory that a certain portion of the manufacturing expense should be applied to the work performed, on the basis of the time that each piece of the product requires of the machines which are necessary to perform the operations. The usual items which are really involved in a machine rate are:

> Depreciation on the machine unit.
> Maintenance and Repairs on the machine unit.
> Power to operate the unit.
> Rent (Cost of floor space occupied).
> Set up Cost.
> Tools (Jigs and Fixtures on Machine).

In this plan of Factory Cost Keeping, the Machine Expense is divided into several dif-

Factory Cost Keeping

ferent groups as seems advisable. Each group contains the machines which incur about the same yearly expense. The machines are numbered the same as for any inventory purpose and have an additional letter or character to identify the group to which they belong. The rate per hour for a machine in any group is the total machine expense of the group divided by the number of machines in the group, and this quotient divided by the number of hours worked in the same period by any machine in question. The following tables show how the rate per hour for any one machine is determined:

Table I—Group Rate

	Group A	Group B	Group C
Number of machines in group..	100	200	75
Machine Expense Per Month per group.................	$14,400	$6,000	$5,000
Share of Expense per Machine........... (Group Expense ÷ No. of Machines)	$144	$30	$66.66

Table II—Hourly Rate—Group A

Number of Machine	Hours Worked	Mo. Exp. per machine in Group A	RATE PER HOUR (Monthly Expense per Machine ÷ Hours worked)
213A	160	$144	$ .90
269A	100	144	1.44
292A	57	144	2.526

Machine Hour Method Modified

17. It is evident that this plan is a just and fair one if the balance of the other expense is distributed correctly. By many it is thought too cumbersome and expensive because the individual machine hours must be collected, which is as complicated as getting individual man hours. In some cases, the group is used as a unit and the total hours for the group is collected, with the rate per hour being the same for each machine in the group. In this modification, very little as regards accuracy and ultimate value of the cost figures is sacrificed but considerable time is saved. However, where the Cost System is planned to use the tabulating machine system, the hours for each machine are collected monthly or semi-monthly at a very small expense and then the hourly rate per machine easily determined.

Value of Machine Hours

18. It will be noted that if individual machine hours are collected and used, it affords the Factory Manager or Superintendent a very good means of control of the idle machine hours, because he can readily get a report showing the total hours worked. This subtracted from the number of working hours gives the idle hours. This knowledge is worth a great deal to the Factory Manager.

Factory Cost Keeping

because idle machine hours form one of the greatest wastes in manufacturing, and many a factory has made increased profits from only a correction of this one condition.

Error of Same Expense in All Departments

19. Where a certain rate of Expense is used to cover all expenses, and all work, regardless of facilities or other conditions, bears a like proportion of this expense, we are confronted with a condition which is not fair to the ultimate consumer and which will not stand competition. To make this plain, let us assume we have a large manufacturing plant composed of several departments, all of which are so equipped that they can produce the same parts or pieces if required. One of these departments, A, is equipped with the ordinary machinery bought in the open market, so that anyone could purchase this same equipment and be on an equal footing with us to turn out the product from these machines. Another department, B, has machines that are bought in the open market, but on which we have put some improvements. Our foreman of this department has so trained his help and systemized his work that we can do twice as much per workman as any of our competitors. Another department, C, has some highly perfected automatic machinery, the product of which has a labor expense of only ¼ of that of any of our competitors.

Estimating Previous Job, If Performed in Department A

20. Now, assuming that (by the Percentage Plan) our expense rate is 100 per cent, we are asked to quote on a piece of work which we decide to make in the first named department, A. We find the expense of material, $50.00 and the Labor Expense, $100.00. To this Labor Expense we add 100 per cent for the Indirect Expenses, making $200.00 or a total of $250.00 manufacturing cost. To this we add $50.00 for Administrative Expense and profit, making the price $300.00, and submit our quotation. We are later informed that a small shop has quoted a price of $240.00 and has been awarded the work. If we met this price we would lose on the job. A little inquiry shows the reason for this—our competitor's business and expenses are small and his Indirect Expense rate is only 50 per cent. This, figuring by the above method, makes his Manufacturing Cost $200.00, leaving him $40.00 for profit and Administrative Expense. If we had been awarded the job at $300.00, we would therefore be charging the customer too much for work done in Department A, when compared to another shop.

Again Estimating Previous Job, If Performed in Department C

21. Again, suppose this work were to be done in the third department, C, and use the same figures. Here our Labor Expense compared to any of our competitors is only 1 to 4 and our competitor would have a $100.00 Labor Expense as before. Adding 50 per cent Indirect Expense to his Labor Expense as before, makes $150.00. Then $50.00 for material, and $40.00 for profit and Administrative Expense, giving a total of $240.00. Compared to this our Labor Expense would be $25.00 with 100 per cent Indirect Expense also giving $25.00, or a total of $50.00. Then $50.00 for material, and $50.00 for profit and Administrative Expense, or a price of $150.00 to the customer for the job. It would be quite evident that we would get the order for this work and the customer a very low price. In reality our price of $150.00 to the customer would not be a profitable job for us to undertake and if we were to do the work for any sustained period, we would soon discover that we were losing money on the job. This loss would be due to the fact that Department C with its costly automatic machinery should carry a much higher Indirect Expense rate than Department A and B. If we were to correct the Indirect Expense rate on Department C, and then re-figure the job, we could probably still offer the customer the lowest bid and receive the job. The price to the customer would be about what he would regularly expect to pay and enable him to make his forecasts accordingly. Further, the corrected estimate would be fair to our competitors.

Departmental Expense

22. The grave danger of estimating costs on a basis of the same Indirect Expense for all departments may be overcome by figuring the Indirect Expense by departments. By this method all departmental expenses such as Supplies, Indirect Wages, and the usual items of Indirect Expense are collected by Departments for a definite period. In addition to the departmental expenses, each department stands its proportionate share of the General Factory Expense on some fair and equitable basis such as floor space, value of equipment, and number of employees. The departmental Indirect Expense plus that department's share of General Factory Expense gives the Total Expense of the Department. This amount divided by the hours worked by the Department within the period selected gives the Departmental Expense Rate per hour. This method gains in favor each year, as it relieves the excessive expense in departments having a small earning power and charges those which have a large earning power in proportion to the use or benefits of the services. It makes each department as

Factory Cost Keeping

though it were a factory itself and its costs should be treated in that manner.

Applying Departmental Expense

23. When a Departmental Expense Rate has been secured as described in the previous paragraph, it is applied to the different products on the basis of time. If product A requires three hours of Direct Labor in the Department, the Departmental Expense Rate is applied by taking three times this rate and adding that amount to the Wages and Material Expenses. If product, B, requires five hours of Direct Labor in the Department, five times the rate is added to the Wages and Material Expenses. In both cases the addition of the amount of Indirect Expense to the Wages and Material gives the total cost within the department. The method of charging Indirect Expense to the product through the medium of a Departmental Expense Rate becomes quite important if there are various lines of product which require more work in one department than in another.

Continuous Production System

24. There are some industries where there is only one product and the Departments are closely related. At such times the Departmental Expense Rate is omitted to save the clerical expense of gathering and dis-

Factory Executive Service

tributing the Indirect Expenses. The entire factory may be treated as one department with a single Indirect Expense Rate. When this latter method is used the system is usually spoken of as a Continuous Production System. Under this System the total of the Expenses is found and divided by the number of units produced within a coincident period in order to find the total cost per unit.

Unit of Product

25. Under any method of determining costs it is necessary to adopt a Unit of Product. Under the Continuous Production Method this Unit will be piece, pound, bushel, ton, yard, etc., as the case may be. Under the Order Cost Method the Order will be the unit. In either case it is necessary to have a Cost Sheet or Cost Card on which is entered the Expense of Material, the Expense of Labor, and the Factory Indirect Expense. The Cost Sheet also sometimes shows the amount of Selling and Administrative Expense to be absorbed and also the Profit or Loss made on the order.

The various methods of distributing generalized groups of expenses, as explained in the foregoing chapter, are all in use at present in many factories, and it is likely that many of our students will be required to conform with them from time to time. However, since none of them are free from serious weaknesses, it is probable that within the relatively near future, a new scientific method will replace them. This new method will analyze product and expenses and make it possible to apply particularized (not generalized) expenses to product in the exact ratios of their utilization. This is worth watching for.

Chapter Eight
ACCURATE COSTS DEPEND UPON ACCURATE TIME RECORDS

The Need for Accurate Original Cost Records

1. The accuracy of any cost system depends entirely upon the accuracy of the original records on which all figures are based. The best cost system ever devised will produce misleading information and jeopardize profits unless all the *basic* records are accurate. Not so long ago the word "costs" as it is used today was unknown. Guesses and rough estimates formed the basis upon which costs were figured. Detail was unheard of in tracing the fabrication of materials, and profits were computed chiefly by an examination of the bank account. Large production, increasing cost of labor, more expensive raw materials, and a realization of the need for accuracy have brought about a rapid change in the manufacturer's attitude toward costs.

Recognition of the Value of Time

2. The recognition of the value of time as a manufacturing ingredient and the increasing cost of labor have made business men more careful of both the purchase and expenditure of man hours. Higher labor costs have served automatically to emphasize the importance of preventing waste time ... eliminating those small minute wastes that creep in unseen and grow rapidly into large money losses.

Relation Between Time and Cost Accounting

3. The checking and regulation of time, therefore, was the fundamental principle upon which cost accounting was built. The recording of employee attendance time . . . the recording of time spent on jobs . . . of the time machines are in operation . . . of the time spent on assembly . . . and numerous other time factors were found to be essential to reliable cost keeping. Under modern operating conditions, no business can afford to overlook the importance of having an exact knowledge of its production costs . . . because of the far reaching effects of even a small amount of lost or waste time.

Time Should Be Controlled as Carefully as Materials

4. The average industrial organization today leaves nothing to chance in its control of materials, but is often less strict in its control of minutes. Every ounce of raw material that comes to the store room is carefully measured, weighed, and checked against invoices to see that full value is received for the money expended. When distributed for production it is again measured with utmost accuracy . . . amounts in process are carefully checked and strict inventories are kept . . . all for the purpose of *preventing loss through waste.*

Yet the cost of material in many industries is small compared to the value of the time required to convert it into finished products . . .

Factory Cost Keeping

and WASTE THROUGH FAILURE TO MEASURE ACCURATELY AND ACCOUNT FOR WORKING MINUTES IS MORE EASILY INCURRED THAN FROM A SIMILAR FAILURE IN THE HANDLING OF MATERIALS. It is not sufficient merely to check the amount of labor time delivered to the plant. It should be handled on exactly the same basis as materials to determine the exact amount received...how much this work costs and what profit it pays.

Workmen Are Not Trained Accountants

5. Pencilled job time memoranda have no place in this day of expensive labor. They are not dependable sources of facts, because workmen, unaccustomed to figuring in fractions, are rarely accurate in accounting for their own time. In most cases where this manual method of accounting is still used, employees wait until the end of the day to make out their work tickets. They must resort to memory because exact times of starting and stopping have not been kept. Round figure guesses on elapsed time are recorded with but one idea in mind ... to account for total time. A full day's pay ... not the employer's manufacturing cost ... is the workman's chief concern. The few minutes here and there charged incorrectly and those minutes not actually used in production help to force a balance, but result in serious distortion of the final cost picture.

Time Records Essential in All Wage Payment Methods

6. Regardless of the method of wage payment, it is essential to profitable management that exact records be kept of the amount of time spent on all jobs. Piece-work, premium, bonus, and differential rates are all based on the time element ... the amount of time required by a capable workman to do a specific amount of work. Burden (or overhead) is usually distributed in proportion to the amount of time spent on each job or phase of work ... a comparatively easy thing to do if every workman adheres exactly to the standard of production set up for his particular kind of work.

In actual practice, however, there are always variations from established standards of production which management cannot ignore if it wants an accurate picture of manufacturing costs upon which to establish selling prices and gauge relative efficiency of individuals, departments, and the plant as a whole.

Consider, for example, the piece-work job that pays one dollar for each one hundred pieces produced. According to pre-determined standards, these one hundred pieces would normally be produced in one hour and the job should absorb the equivalent of one hour's burden. If the workman is inefficient and requires two hours to accomplish this task, the direct labor cost does not increase, but because

Factory Cost Keeping

manufacturing expense goes on continuously, two hours of burden instead of one must be added to the cost of the job. This, obviously, increases the final cost of the product.

TIME IS USUALLY A CONTROLLING FACTOR DETERMINING THE PROPORTION OF OVERHEAD EXPENSE EACH JOB SHOULD ABSORB.

6a. The plant that keeps accurate job cost records is protected by current knowledge of all variations from its production standards ... and management takes advantage of this knowledge by making whatever adjustments are necessary to insure a uniform margin of profit.

Payroll Time and Job Time

7. Payroll time is the total amount of time purchased from employees and is similar to the bulk delivery of materials. Job cost time corresponds to the material requisitioned for specific jobs ... it is the number of minutes actually used in productive work, or the amount of time that becomes available for resale at a profit. The difference between payroll time and job cost time represents money expended for which no return may be expected. Unlike wasted and unused materials which can be at least partially recovered, wasted and unused minutes cannot be- salvaged. There is no scrap price for waste minutes ... they must be accepted as outright money losses and written out of profits. When

Factory Executive Service

total minutes used fails to agree with total minutes bought, the inevitable result is higher costs, and reduced profits.

Control of Time

8. Accuracy in Cost Records begins with the control of the workers' time throughout a factory and office. A self-regulating time system is the proper means of measuring time in industrial establishments. This type of system, with a master time control which is regulated automatically by a synchronous motor, provides an automatic means of controlling the money-value of labor time. Figure 8a illustrates such a master time control. This central control or master time control is completely self-supervising without manual regulation. Vibration, temperature, humidity, or barometric pressure will not affect its accuracy. All the indicating and recording units, such as wall clocks, time stamps, attendance time and job cost recorders, which are included in the self-regulating system, are checked automatically every hour with the accurate time of the control unit. This unit will operate an electric time system year in and year out within a few seconds of correct time. If the power supply is interrupted, the master time control will continue to run for as long as 12 hours. With this type of system installed, uniform time on all time recording, indicating, and signaling equipment is assured.

Attendance Recorders

9. Several popular systems of securing attendance records are on weekly, bi-weekly

NO. 107
NAME Jane Spencer
WEEK ENDING 3/27 19___

R.T. HOURS	RATE	AMOUNT	WITHHOLDING TAX	WITHHOLDING TAX CLASS
40	1.10	44.00	4.60	2
O.T. HOURS	RATE	AMOUNT	FEDERAL O.A.S.I.	TOTAL EARNINGS
3	1.65	4.95	.49	48.95
HOURS		AMOUNT	STATE U.C.	TOTAL DEDUCTIONS
43		48.95		8.84
		TAX EXEMPT	BONDS	BALANCE DUE
			3.75	
		TAXABLE BAL.		40.11

DAY	MORNING IN	MORNING OUT	AFTERNOON IN	AFTERNOON OUT	OVERTIME IN	OVERTIME OUT	HRS.
1	SU 8 00	SU 12 00	SU 1 00	SU 4 58			8
2	MO 8 00	MO 12 02	MO 12 59	MO 5 03			8
3	TU 7 59	TU 12 01	TU 1 00	TU 5 01			8
4	WE 7 57	WE 12 00	WE 12 57	WE 5 02	WE 5 30	WE 8 34	11
5	FR 8 18	FR 12 02	FR 12 59	FR 5 00			8
6							
7							

TOTAL TIME 43

Jane Spencer
SIGNATURE

FIGURE 3. *Weekly Attendance Record Card. Used where employees arrive and depart on scheduled hours.*

[59]

Factory Executive Service

or semi-monthly cards. The period of record corresponds with the payroll period which has been adopted in the particular factory. When an employee comes to work, he removes his individual card from its place in

Figure 4. *Weekly Attendance Record Card. Used where employees arrive and depart at different times of the day.*

FACTORY COST KEEPING

the "Out" rack and inserts it in the time recorder which automatically prints the date or day, hour and minute of arrival. This becomes an exact register of the time the workman reported for duty. The card is then placed in

FIGURE 5. *Installation of Time Recorder and Card Racks showing employee "registering in" at 8:18 a. m.*

Factory Executive Service

the "In" rack by the individual and remains there until he registers out at the regular quitting time or when he leaves for the day. Figures 3 and 4 are reproductions of attendance record cards for regular or irregular working schedules. Figure 5 shows an installation of card racks and attendance time recorder with an employee in the act of registering "In" at 8:18 a. m. Figure 8 is another type of Attendance Time Recorder enclosed in a metal case.

When electric accounting machines are used for payroll and labor cost accounting (see Chapter IX), a punched card can be used for the clock card. The clock registrations can be printed either on the face or reverse side of the card and, in addition, the card can be designed for recording. In this case, the card is designed to provide for clock rings as well as the spaces for recording the various jobs performed by the workman during the day. The card above illustrates such registrations on the back of a Daily Reporting Card and its use is shown later in this chapter.

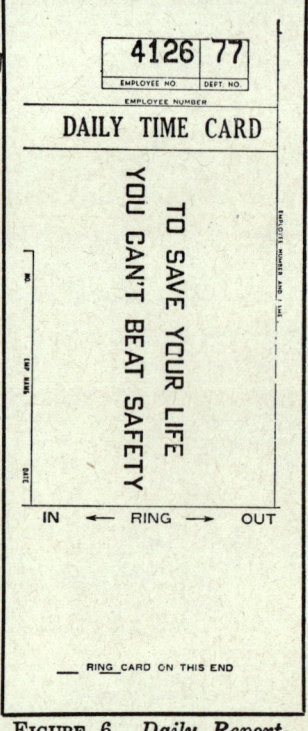

FIGURE 6. *Daily Reporting Time Card.*

[62]

FACTORY COST KEEPING

9a. Many factories use an attendance record card recorder called the Payroll Dial Recorder. This large machine which is of earlier design is still in use in many factories today. It gives the attendance record in the form of a large sheet of rolled paper. The advantages of this older dial type recorder have been surpassed by the new Attendance Time Recorder, Figure 8. This is shown with the older dial type. The dial type is still manufactured and sold—and preferred by some companies having low payroll turnover. The compact, highly reliable Attendance Time Recorder is rapidly being adopted by modern factories.

FIGURE 7. *Payroll Dial Recorder.*

FIGURE 8. *Attendance Time Recorder.*

9b. It was once satisfactory to have the employees register their attendance cards as they entered the plant. If a man registered on time, it was several minutes later before he arrived at his department. This resulted in the employees being paid for time that they did not work. To save these minutes each day, industry is now installing the time

Factory Executive Service

recorders, singly or in groups, either in the departments or at stations conveniently located near the departments. An employee thus has to register "In" in his department to receive an "On Time" registration.

9c. Both the card type and the payroll dial type of recorder are provided with an automatic two color auditing feature. With this feature all regular or "On Time" registrations are recorded in blue ink and all "Tardy" or "Early Out" registrations are recorded in red ink. Overtime is likewise indicated in a red imprint. Aside from the fact that the moral effect of the red record tends to bring the employees in "on time," the red imprint makes checking of the records much easier for the time clerk.

The accuracy of the foregoing procedure depends upon the smooth operation of the master time and program control. The illustration shows an advanced design of such an instrument. It is a precision movement which needs no pendulum. It is regulated automatically by a synchronous motor, all of which makes the accuracy of time recording a foregone conclusion. The Time Clerk is thus certain of the precision of his records.

FIGURE 8a. *Master Time and Program Control.*

The Time Clerk

10. The Attendance Record Cards are usually supervised by the departmental time clerk or a foreman. He sees that new cards are in their numbered places in the rack when a pay period begins. If an employee fails to register "In" or "Out," the time clerk or foreman investigates the case, and corrects the Attendance Record Card only with an O. K. from the Chief Time Clerk or Superintendent of the department. It usually is the time clerk's duty to see that the time on the Attendance Record Card and Job Cost Cards agree as to the totals for each working period or shift. At the end of the day or pay period, the time clerk totals the hours worked and makes that entry on the card before turning it into the Payroll Department. If a new man has lost time in coming through the Employment

FIGURE 9. *Two examples of Modern Time Stamps which can be used by Foremen and Superintendents to punch special time cards.*

Department but is to be given credit for starting at the opening hour, his time card is marked and O.K.'d by the Superintendent as though the man started at opening time. Where a time clock system is used, it is always a Company rule that no employee touches another employee's card to ring "In" or "Out" for the other individual. If for some reason a workman should have credit for starting on time but is not there in person to ring his card, the Superintendent can later in the day or pay period O.K. the starting time.

Job Cost Cards

11. The Time Clerk, floor checker, or foreman, makes out a Job Card that covers the particular job or operation to which the workman is assigned. In some cases, the Job Card is made out in the Planning Department as a part of the Dispatching of Production. The Job Card accompanies the work into the department in such cases and when an individual is assigned to the task, his clock number, name and other facts are entered on the card to complete it. A study of Figures 11 and 12 reveals two distinct kinds of Job Cards, namely, Daily and Period Job Cards. Direct and Indirect Labor are sometimes further distinguished by being printed on different colored stock or on cards with different colored stripes at the top of the face of the card.

With the electric punched-card accounting machine installation in a factory for collecting costs, the Job Cost Cards are made out on standard forms that are a part of the system which is described in the following Chapter. Figures 11 and 12 shows typical Job Cards.

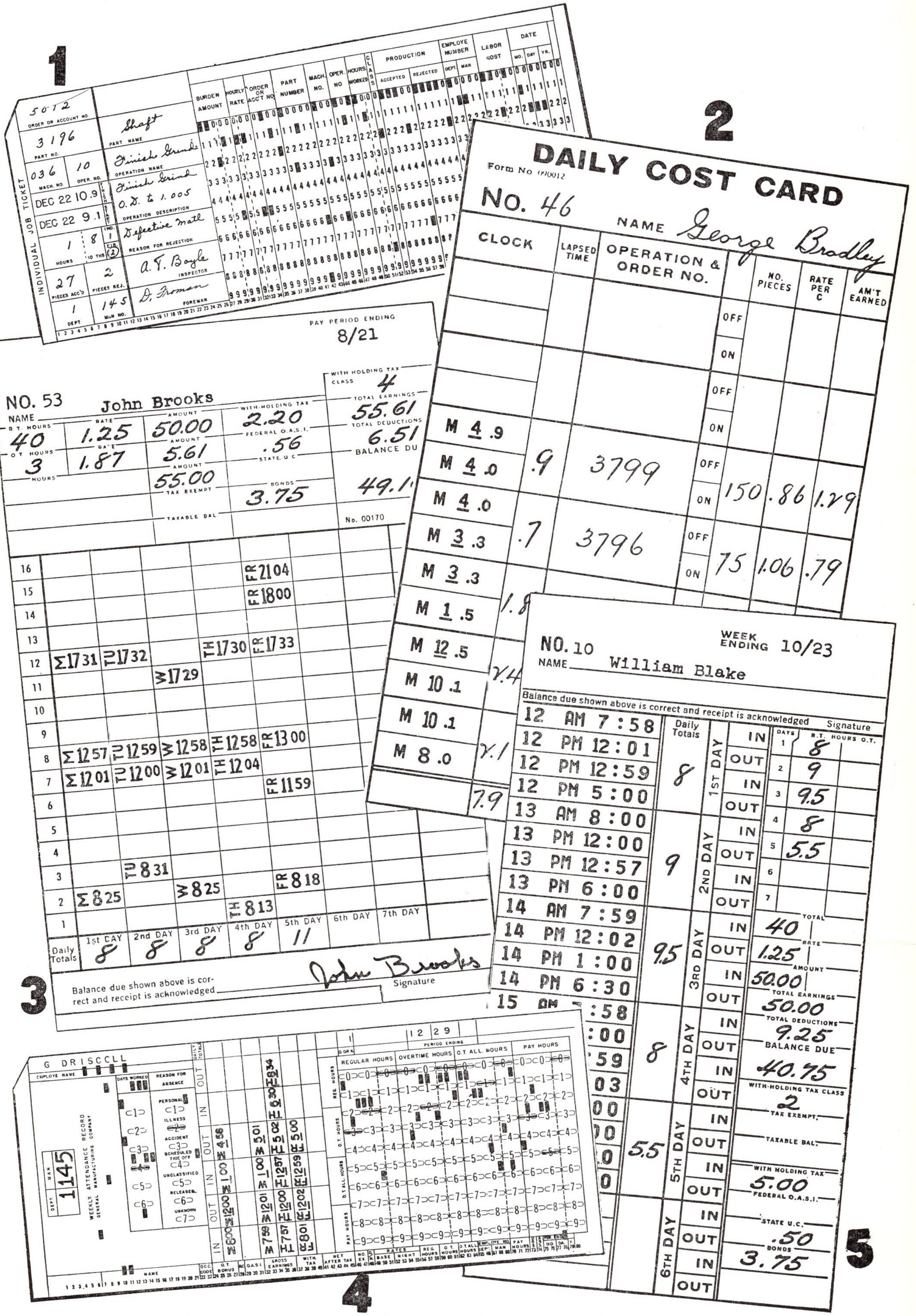

FIGURE 10. *A group of Cost Card forms, used in collecting Cost Data, which shows several positions of time registrations. See back of page for card descriptions.*

1. One form of an Individual Job Ticket or Card.
2. A Daily Cost Card produced by a Job Cost Recorder.
3. An Attendance Time Record produced on an Attendance Time Recorder, Figure Eight.
4. A form of a Payroll Accounting Card.
5. An Attendance Time Record produced on a Job Cost (Time) Recorder, Figure 10a.

Information on Job Cards

12. While the details of the Direct Labor Job Cards vary to fit the industry or particular factory, there are some points of information that one finds covered on the face side of nearly all job cards. Factory provision is made on nearly all job cards for recording some of the following types of information:

Employee's Name	Job Number or
Employee's Number	Order Number
Department Number	Operation Number
Account Number	Machine Number
Standard Cost	Standard Hours
Hourly Rate	Elapsed Hours
Total Amount	Hours Saved
Actual Cost	Set Up Time
Expense Rate	Piece Work Price
Expense Amount	Number of Pieces

12a. In connection with the Job Cards, there is provision for printing a clock registration at the time of starting the job and time of stopping for the job or for the day. Where the jobs are of such nature that they are completed in several hours or within any one day, only two spaces for clock rings are required—Start and Stop. In the case of jobs that run for several days or where the individual works much of the time at Indirect Labor charged to the same Expense Account, the back of the Job Cards is used for the additional clock rings.

Job Cost Recorders

13. The Job Cost Recorder is one of the units that insures the collection of accurate cost data in the sense that it authenticates the time element on all jobs for all employees. The best recorder is an electric machine that is a part of the entire time clock system and is fully controlled by a master time control. Figure 10a shows a popular type of Job Cost Recorder which becomes hourly - supervised when wired into the self-regulating time sys-

FIGURE 10a. *Two types of modern job cost recorders.*

tem. Job Recorders connected to Master Clock, can be set to print 0.0 at Starting Time in the morning.

Throughout the day the Job Cost Recorder records the elapsed time and hours and tenths, or in hours and hundredths, so that when the stopping time on a job is recorded, the elapsed time can be determined by simple subtraction of the starting time from the stopping time.

Factory Cost Keeping

All non-working periods such as noon lunch hour are automatically eliminated through a program device. This facilitates the checking of the job records in the cost department. For single units or for isolated units that may be more or less temporary, this type of Job Cost Recorder may be operated by connecting to the alternating current circuit by plugging into a light socket or wall plug. This recording device is driven by an electric motor powered directly from the lighting circuit.

13a. On the Job Time Card the Recorder prints the actual starting and stopping time on jobs. There is no chance of error as there is from a lead pencil memorandum. The Recorder prints on any form of cost card to meet the particular requirements of the factory cost system, and on either right or left margin of the card. The guide mark directly below the clock face, indicates the correct printing position and insures all the registrations of all time entries falling in their proper places. The time of stopping a job is always printed above the time of starting, as:

STOP	Sept. 4	11.7
START	Sept. 4	7.0
	Elapsed Hours	4.7

This simplifies the subtractions necessary to determine the elapsed hours and tenths worked on the job. The printed time is indisputable and furnishes to the Cost Department a legible record that workmen, foreman, su-

Factory Executive Service

perintendent and clerks in the Cost Department all know to be correct. Figure 10 shows a group of different designs of card forms used in collecting cost data and illustrates various positions of the time registrations. Some of these are used directly in electric punched card sorting and accounting machines are being punched, whereas the information on cards of other shapes and sizes is designed for various manual methods of collecting cost and payroll data. In the former instance, however, facts are recorded only once in punched cards. The cards are then processed automatically by electric punched-card accounting machines to prepare various accounting reports.

CHAPTER NINE

COLLECTING COSTS WITH THE AID OF MACHINES

Use of Machines in Offices

1. Automatic machinery and machine tools have been introduced into the various manufacturing departments of all businesses in order to produce a greater volume of manufactured articles in a shorter period of time, to eliminate the elements of delay and waste usually attendant to manual methods, and to produce manufactured articles at a lower cost to the manufacturer. Automatic machinery likewise has been introduced into the offices of business in general for a somewhat similar purpose. It is equally important that the manufacturer should know the cost of each article he manufactures and this should be accomplished by introducing automatic machinery, which will aid in analyzing quickly, accurately and comprehensively, at the least expense, the various facts relating to costs, which will permit him to market his products at a profit.

Electric Punched Card Accounting Machine Method

2. Progressive manufacturers of today are employing Electric Punched Card Accounting Machines to secure accurate, timely and detailed reports, vital to the conduct of their businesses. These machines are nothing more or less than machine tools with which to

Factory Executive Service

secure Payroll, Material, Wages, Sales, Indirect Expenses and Distributions and other accounting and statistical reports, by which the manufacturer is enabled to control the various activities in a plant as these affect the profits of the business.

The Punched Card

3. The Tabulating Card is almost identical in appearance with any other form for reporting time or labor. When the electric accounting or punched card method is introduced, the only requirement, insofar as the original entry in the shop is concerned, is that labor be reported on a time card or job ticket of a standard size ($7\frac{3}{8}$" by $3\frac{1}{4}$") and thickness, so that it will ultimately feed through the machines by which the various reports will be prepared. Among the various designs of cards on which to report Labor and Time in the shop departments are the following:

1—The Job Card (Figure 11)
2—The Continuous Job Card (Figure 12)
3—The Daily Reporting Card (Figure 13)

The Job Card

4. A card similar to Figure 11 is designed when a concern requires that a separate card be used to report each job performed by each workman each day. The design of the card and facts recorded are determined by individual requirements. This is a dual card, providing a columnar arrange-

Factory Cost Keeping

ment for reproducing in terms of punched holes, all the data recorded on the card by the

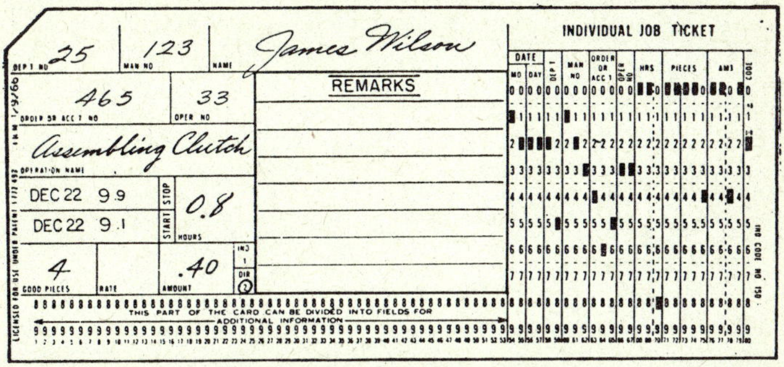

FIGURE 11. *Individual Job Card.**

Foreman, Time Clerk, or Workman in the shop. The columns in the card are numbered consecutively from 1 to 80 inclusive. The "fields" on the card in which the various data are recorded may be identified by the captions: Clock No., Order No., Hours, Pieces, Amount, Department, and Machine.

The Continuous Job Card

5. A Continuous Job Card, Figure 12, is designed usually when a job is planned through to completion in a Planning Department. These cards usually originate in the Planning Department and the data is filled in completely before the card reaches the shop except for the Date, Employee Number, etc., which is then noted thereon by the foreman or workman. The card remains with the job

*The words "ticket" and "card" are used to mean the same thing.

Factory Executive Service

until completion or until the end of the pay period. At either of these times the sum-

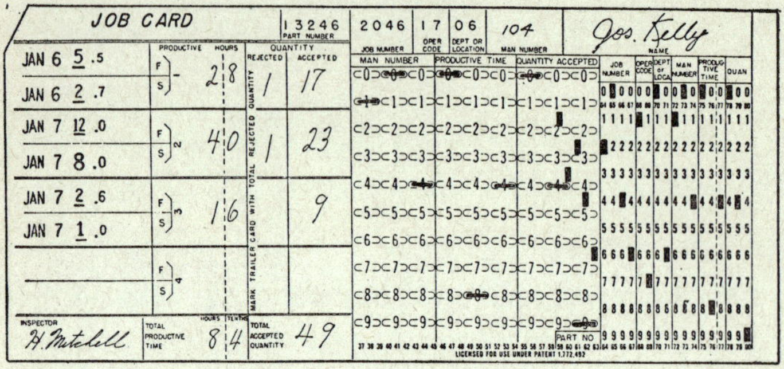

FIGURE 12. *Continuous Job Card.*

maries of Hours, Pieces, and Amounts are entered on the card. Provision is made on this type of card, Figure 12, for recording the various times a workman starts and stops on the job, by some standard job recorder as described in the previous chapter. The student will note the series of clock registrations on the left edge of the card, covering a period of three days.

The Daily Reporting Card

6. The Daily Reporting Card, Figure 13, differs from the other types of job cards, Figures 11 and 12, in that only one card is headed and used each day by the workman.

When the employee is employed, he is assigned a clock number for identification and is issued an attendance clock card. The clock card may be either "daily" or "pay period."

Factory Cost Keeping

This card is used to determine (1) the time the employee works for the employer and (2) the amount earned.

Daily, or at the end of the pay period, the attendance time is figured and entered on the clock card, either by writing in the boxes pro-

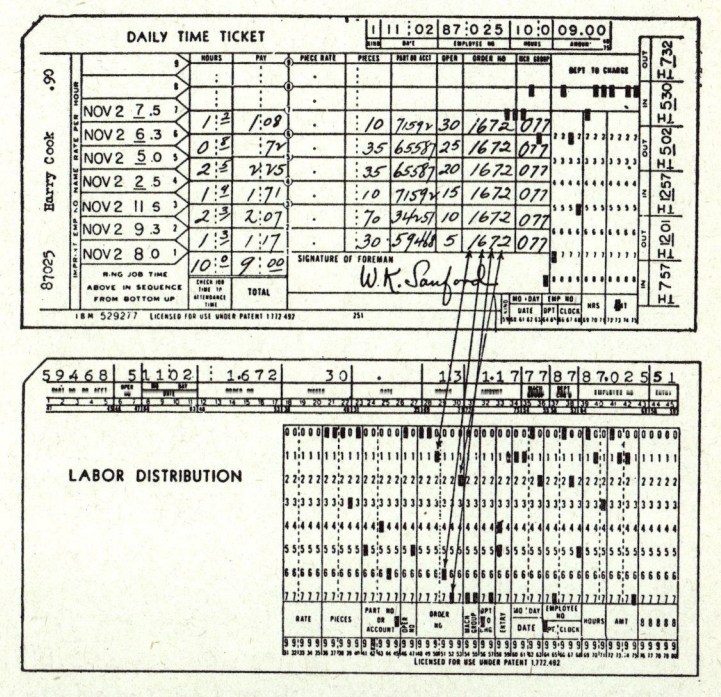

FIGURE 13. *A Daily Time (Reporting) Card shown with its Trailer Card below. The Trailer card is punched from the Daily Time Card.*

vided or by marking corresponding digits which are then punched by an automatic machine.

[75]

Factory Executive Service

Each day, or as they are received, the attendance and job time cards are punched, and all information needed for both the payroll and the labor distribution reports is transferred into the accounting machine cards in the form of punched holes.

A record of all jobs performed during the day by a workman is recorded on this single card. This form of reporting, insofar as the shop is concerned, entails less clerical work on the part of the factory personnel. This also presents an easier method of accounting for time. The routine when the above cards reach the Cost Department will be covered in later paragraphs.

The Trailer Card is a card to which is transcribed, by means of punched holes, the pertinent data concerning one order number, department, operation, etc., appearing on a card such as the daily time card. For example, the several cards punched from the daily time card to distribute the job time reported thereon would be called trailer cards.

6a. Another form of job card is the Gang Job Ticket or Card. They are used when a job requires the services of more than a single workman. Although they contain the same information as individual job tickets, they differ from individual job tickets in that they contain also the employee number, hours, and amounts for each operator participating in the work.

Factory Cost Keeping

Gang Job Tickets look very much like the Individual Job Card, Figure 11, except that there is sufficient space allotted for entering the names of more than one employee. From the gang job tickets, supplementary cards are punched, one for each employee. The latter cards are used to tabulate the payroll, and the gang job tickets for distribution and cost purposes.

6b. The Daily Time (Reporting) Card is used directly in the calculation of labor distribution and such analyses as are necessary for effective current labor control. The supplementary labor distribution trailer cards are tabulated daily in making up such analyses as the Direct Labor Cost Analysis shown in the figure 13a. The totals shown on the Trailer cards are also balanced with the total of the payroll cards. The daily time reports are filed until the end of the pay period. The direct distribution cards are placed in the work-in-process cost file, and the indirect labor cards in an expense labor distribution file. From these records the Analysis shown in the Figure 13a is checked. Note how the information from the Daily Time Card (Ticket) is transferred to the Trailer card by the Reproducing Punch (Figure 14) and thence to the Direct Labor Cost Analysis. Figure 13a is a good example of how these forms correlate with each other and how one form is made up from another.

In some cases the distribution (trailer)

Factory Executive Service

cards are sorted with the payroll cards by man number, and listed on a report generally called the Payroll and Distribution Register. See Figure 21. In other cases, the payroll cards and the distribution cards are separated after the balancing operation and the Registers are listed separately. In most cases the Registers are usually prepared for each pay period.

Punching of Perforations

7. The holes which have been perforated into these cards are a reproduction in terms of numerical codes of the various items and data which have been written on the card in the shop. A rather homely simile is that of the player piano roll, in which perforations have been made for the purpose of playing a tune when the roll is fed through the piano. The 80 column cards are punched with rectangular holes about 1/16" wide and ⅛" high. The punched cards like those illustrated, ultimately are fed through the Electric Punched Card Sorting, and accounting as well as auxiliary machines. These machines by means of electrical contacts made through punched holes in the cards, will produce the various payroll and labor distribution reports. The locations of the holes in the vertical columns are determined by the amounts or code of the data to be punched. The caption determines the column or groups of columns, termed a "field," within which each code classification or amount is punched.

The Electric End Printing Reproducing Punch

7a. This is a newly developed electrically operated punching machine which utilizes electronic principles to do its work. This automatic punch is capable of translating punched holes such as those shown in Figures 11, 12 and 13 into printed figures on the same, or a duplicate of that card. It will transcribe and record electronically from a pencil marked entry such as shown in the Man Number, Productive Time and Quantity Accepted columns in Figure 12. Recorded data taken from one group of cards to another is easily duplicated by this machine. It also transfers codes and other data from a master card to associated detail cards. The machine checks the accuracy of its operation while preparing a duplicate set of cards, or in another concurrent step when transferring data from master to detail cards. This new reproducing punch will record totals, summaries and bal-

FIGURE 14. *Electric End Printing Reproducing Punch Machine.*

FACTORY EXECUTIVE SERVICE

ances brought forward in conjunction with an Electric Punched Card Accounting Machine.

The Electric Card Punching Machine

8. The written information on the various types of punched cards, as illustrated before, is permanently recorded in terms of punched holes by the Electric Card Punching machine, Figure 15. This punching is usually done in the same department where the other machines of the system are installed. Economy and accuracy are obtained by means of automatic card feeding and ejecting, and electric keyboard operation.

The operator cuts the perforation into the card representing the various data by depressing the various keys in the keyboard of the machine. The number of cards so punched, per hour, depends upon the amount of information necessary to perforate on a card, the legibility of the original data and the skill of the operator. An average speed is 2000 to 3000 cards per day. There are several types of

FIGURE 15. *The Electric Card Punching Machine.*

[80]

DIRECT LABOR COST ANALYSIS

PERIOD ENDING _____

PART NUMBER	OPERATION NO.	PIECES	HOURS	AMOUNT	TOTAL HOURS	TOTAL AMOUNT
2685 2685 2685 2685	12 14 16 18	2500 2405 2431 2318	1829 1963 1852 2246 1108	9460 8575 5200 9065 5597	7998 *	37897 *
2689 2689 2689	14 15 16	1185 1180 1180	456 485 413	2255 2936 2015	1354 *	7206 *
12432	12	2450	1839	9514	1839 *	9514 *
19241 19241	12 15	385 385 320	558 558 242	3680 3214 1673	1358 *	8567 *
19264 19264	18 21 22	835 835 650	923 961 489	5905 6295 6240	2373 *	14600 *
19925 19925 19925	23 24 32	1008 998 994	540 532 516	3250 3418 3185	2109 *	11973 *
21237 21237 21237	14 16 119	3650 2055 3425	428 413 408 438	2648 2849 2464 2598	*1688 *	10559 *
28352 28352	12 14	182 1180	1218 113	2400 2257 3045	397 *	8202 *
28353 28353 28353	18 21 32	21842 20250 20150	2126 1980 1982	10265 9745 9599	6091 *	29609 *
59468 59468 59468	13 5	300 300	103 231 531	2206 2140 6150	857 *	10500 *
					26064 *	148627 *

FIGURE 13a. *Illustrating the transfer of card information to a direct labor cost analysis sheet.*

Factory Cost Keeping

Electric Card Punching Machines, identical in purpose but differing slightly in certain features. Some machines record only numerical information while others record both numerical and alphabetical data.

8a. The duplicating feature of the electric card punching machine provides for automatically punching or copying such information as date, department, etc., which is common to a large group of cards. This operation is performed automatically by the punch itself from a master set-up without the aid of the operator.

Electric Punched Hole Verifier

8b. The Electric Punched Hole Verifier is used to verify the punching of cards while still in the same sequence as the source documents. Accuracy of records and reports is assured by the single verification of the original transcription of information and by balancing report totals against accounting controls. A new development is a verifier which provides greater speed, flexibility, and ease of operation in verifying data punched in cards. When a card has been verified satisfactorily, the machine cuts a notch into its top edge, affording a permanent and visible proof of verification.

The Electric Punched Card Sorting Machine

9. The Electric Punched Card Sorting machine is a motor driven machine into which

FACTORY EXECUTIVE SERVICE

the cards are fed from a magazine at a rate of four hundred and fifty per minute. The purpose of this machine is to arrange automatically the cards into any desired groups, such as Employee Number for payroll purposes, or to assemble the cards by Order Number or Account Number, for labor distribution purposes.

FIGURE 16. *The Electric Punched Card Sorting Machine.*

The machine is arranged with thirteen pockets numbered respectively R X 0 1 2 3 4 5 6 7 8 9 and "Reject." One digit of a sorting field is assorted at one time, with the cards being directed to their proper pocket by an electric contact through the hole in the column which is being assorted. For instance, if we were sorting on the unit column of the Employee Number field, a card punched "Employee No. 352" would be directed into the "2" box because a "2 hole" would be punched in the unit position of the field. Likewise, this same card being sorted, from within a group by the tens digit, would be directed into the "5" box, because a "5 hole" is punched in the tens digit of the Employee Number field. Figure 16 illustrates the machine.

[82]

Electric Punched Card Accounting Machine

10. There are many types of punched card accounting machines, from which a selection may be made by the factory executive, in accordance with the requirements of the business. The general function of these machines, as applied to factory accounting, is to produce Payrolls and Cost Reports as to Department, Employee No., Order No., Part No., Operation Account, Pieces, Hours, Amount, etc., after the cards have been sorted in the required sequence. The accounting machine likewise, adds these totals by electrical contact through the holes representing these quantities and money values, which have been punched into the cards. A variety of different factors such as Actual Hours, Standard Hours, Pieces, Actual Earnings, and Standard Earnings, can be tabulated simultaneously on all types of tabulating machines.

This machine reads the cards and positions multiple — copy forms simultaneously at high speed; records the information, adds or subtracts; accumulates and prints many combinations of totals. Figure 17 illustrates an Electric Punched Card Account-

FIGURE 17. *The Punching Card Accounting Machine.*

Factory Executive Service

ing Machine. Figure 18 shows a typical Accounting Machine installation in the offices of a large company.

FIGURE 18.

10a. A brief description of one type accounting machine is as follows:

The Type 405 Electric Punched Card Accounting Machine may be used to list both alphabetical and numerical details from every punched card or from selected punched cards. It also may be used to accumulate and print the various classifications of totals. All such compilations can be printed automatically as finished reports with complete descriptive information.

Factory Cost Keeping

Cards are listed at the rate of 80 cards per minute; they are accumulated without listing at either 80 or 150 cards per minute depending on the model. The machine is equipped with major, intermediate, and minor controls which provide for the printing of group totals when classifications change. Succeeding groups are accumulated without attention from the operator.

The machine is equipped with a removable Control Panel, which enables it to interpret the data on the cards in any desired manner. Two types of panels are available: *Manual,* which provides for convenient changes by the operator; and *fixed,* which allows a permanent arrangement but may be changed if desired.

The type 921 Automatic Carriage increases the number of applications for the accounting machine. It provides for the automatic use of continuous forms for document-writing and report preparation.

In addition to the basic types of machines, there are several other types which facilitate accounting. For example, the Calculating Punch which reads factors from punched cards, performs calculations, and then punches results for individual cards or groups of cards. The machine automatically adds or subtracts factors in the same card; multiplies, divides, or performs all these operations in combination. It calculates earnings, taxes, averages, rates, percentages, and many other single or multiple results for problems in payroll, labor, cost, and other accounting. The Electric Punched Card Interpreter prints punched data in neat, legible characters across the top edge of the card in any sequence to facilitate reference. These and many other automatic machines insure speed and accuracy in producing general accounting and cost accounting reports.

Value of Electric Punched Card Accounting Machines

11. The chief value of the electric punched card accounting equipment exists obviously in its tremendous: (1) Speed, (2) Accuracy, (3) Flexibility, (4) Economy. Under manual methods, in order to produce and control the various cost records required by a business, it is necessary to prepare detail sheets, with necessary headings, under which to post daily by hand, the various items which are to be accumulated into final cost and payroll totals. Under the electric accounting method, the transcription of the original entry into terms of punched holes on the electric accounting card, eliminates the necessity for any and all daily postings to all these various forms. It will be seen that these cards may be accumulated until the end of the analysis period and then, may be quickly and accurately assorted and tabulated according to what is punched thereon, without the necessity of posting daily to any manual records.

Scope of Use of Electric Accounting Machine Systems

12. The installation of the tabulating machine method enables the Factory Cost Accountant to present accurate and complete cost data to the factory executives and so promptly that cost tendencies can be controlled at all times. The accounting machine systems are used to serve a factory in a great many ways. The following are some of the many uses of the electric accounting machine system in cost accounting.

1—Costs
—Regular Product, Parts, Order Operation, Special Jobs, by Departments, etc.
—Analyzing Expense Detail by Accounts and Departments.
—Preparing Exhibits of Comparative Costs.
—Monthly Closing Entries.

2—Payrolls
THE ELECTRIC ACCOUNTING METHOD MECHANIZES ALL THESE PAYROLL OPERATIONS . . .

A. Prepare Payroll Source Records
—Attendance Time Cards
—Job Time Cards
—Deduction Cards
—Employee Withholding Tax Exemption Certificates (W-4)

B. Compute the Payroll
—Reconciliation of Attendance Time with Job Time
—Rate and Extensions of Job Time

Factory Executive Service

- —Extensions of Regular and Overtime Earnings
- —Night Shift Bonus
- —Production Bonus
- —Withholding Tax
- —Old Age and Survivors' Insurance
- —Unemployment Compensation Insurance
- —Retirement Deduction
- —Bond Deduction
- —Net Pay
- —Denomination of Cash Payroll

C. Write the Payroll
- —Payroll Register
- —Earnings Statement and Deduction Receipt
- —Pay Check or Envelope
- —Employee Earnings Record to Date

D. Distribute the Payroll
- —War Bond Accounting
- —Deduction Registers
- —Direct and Indirect Labor Analyses
- —Absentee and Lost Time Report
- —Overtime Analysis
- —Shift Efficiency Report
- —Labor Efficiency Reports
- —Labor Cost Budgets
- —Job Order Costs
- —Piece Work Analysis
- —Standard Cost Comparisons
- —Analysis of Defective Work
- —Production Reports
- —Machine Efficiency Reports
- —Check Reconciliation
- —Wage Statistics
- —Personnel Statistics
- —Seniority Reports
- —Personnel Appraisal Reports
- —Payroll Stabilization Reports
- —Workmen's Compensation Reports
- —State U.C.I. Report

- —Federal O.A.S.I. Report (SS-1A) (SS-1B)
- —State Income Tax Report
- —Annual Federal Report of Tax Withheld (W-2), (W-3)
- —Auditing Employees' Earnings
- —Employees' Payroll Checks or Envelopes
- —Distribution of Payroll Charges, Direct and Indirect Wages
- —Analysis as by Day Work, Piece Work, Day, Night, Male, Female, Bonus and Wage Incentive Tabulations.

3—Materials
- —Distribution of Material Costs.
- —Controlling Material Ordered, Received, Disbursed.

4—Distribution of Expense
- —Accrued Expense by Departments, Compiling Expense, Wages and Material for Determining Total Indirect Expense.

5—Depreciation Accounts
- —Plant and Equipment Records.

6—Inventories
- —Materials.
- —Work-in-process.
- —Warehouse Stock and Finished Products.
- —Equipment.
- —Physical Inventories.

Besides Cost Data, other information of importance in the control of the factory can be had from a series of card forms designed for particular situations. The following is a partial list of various factors on which information can be furnished in usable form and very promptly:

1—Production
- —Reports by Periods, by Departments.
- —Statements of Machine Hours.

Factory Executive Service

   —Labor Efficiency.
   —Scrap.
   —Defective Material.
   —Re-operations.
   —Record of Idle Time by Departments, Machine, and Cause.
2—Personnel Records
3—Analyses of Sales and Advertising
   —Sales Expense, by Products, Departments, Salesmen, Districts, States, Counties, and Cities.
4—Completed Orders
   —Compiling Hours,, Amounts, Material and Indirect Expense.
   —Final Cost Sheets.

Reports Developed by Tabulating Machine Methods

13. The next three paragraphs are presented to show specific reports and cost exhibits that may be developed with the aid of the Electric Accounting Machine method.

13a.—Expense Records. Figure 19 illustrates a tabulation of Wages on a completed order (No. 13695). It will be noted that the cards covering the wages to be charged to this Order Number have been removed from an "In-Process" File and have been assorted by the sorting machines into a sequence of Part Number by Operation. When the cards on the Order Number have been assorted, they are placed in the Electric Accounting Machine which will produce the Expense Record illustrated in Figure 19. It will be noted that totals of Pieces, Hours, and Amounts, are produced for each operation on each Part Number, and

EXPENSE RECORD

ORDER NO. 13695

PART NO.	OPERATION NO.	NO. OF PIECES	OPERATION		PARTS	
			HOURS	AMOUNT	HOURS	AMOUNT
3210	2	620	7 11	39 53		
3210	3	310	2 82	15 27		
3210	5	308	1 65	9 22		
3210	6	308	91	5 17		
3210	12	305	89	6 70		
3210	24	305	99	4 86		
3210	33	304	1 09	5 02		
3210	90	304	59	3 07		
					16 05 *	88 84 *
3220	4	619	7 08	41 42		
3220	6	305	28	1 12		

MATERIAL CHARGES

✓ PRODUCTION ORDERS
  EXPENSE ACCOUNTS   MONTH OF

DEPT. CHGD.	ORDER OR ACC'T. No.	MAT'L. CLASS	STOCK OR PART No.	QUANTITY	AMOUNT	TOTAL AMOUNT
4	109367	301	10300	120	29 05	
14	109367	301	10300	25	5 05	
4	109367	301	10300	832	201 43	
1	109367	301	20400	756	1041 84	
1	109367	301	29648	13	76 58	
2	109367	305	20012	10	5 15	
2	109367	305	40834	27	210 25	
2	109367	305	40834	45	350 41	
12	109367	305	50945	7	69 87	
12	109367	320	10106	15 CR	5 19 CR	
12	109367	320	10204	30	11 04	
12	109367	320	10204	319	117 39	
12	109367	320	30301	15	3 23	
12	109367	320	30301	93	20 01	
12	109367	320	30301	14	3 01	
23	109367	355	10207	15 CR	7 54 CR	
						2132 58 *
2	109368	301	10300	10	2 42	

DIRECT LABOR SUMMARY
CLASSIFIED BY ORDER AND PART NUMBER

ORDER NO	PART NO	OPER. NO.	PIECES	HOURS	AMOUNT
5012	3196	8	100	36 5	34 70
	3196	10	98	14 3	13 85
				50 8 *	48 55 *
5039	4748	3	60	2 7	2 95
	4748	47	59	47 8	55 10
	4748	82	59	12 5	14 10
				63 0 *	72 15 *
5076	7236	7	14	19 9	21 38
	7236	29	7	3 7	3 97
	7236	64	29	72 0	74 65
	7236	74	26	12 3	13 73
				107 9 *	113 73 *
5173	7639	14	94	40 8	41 28
	7639	16	52	8 6	9 30
	7639	53	66	43 5	44 90
				92 9 *	95 48 *
5437	8694	2	46	23 7	24 35
	8694	19	29	69 1	70 14
				92 8 *	94 49 *

FIGURE 19. *Illustrating examples of a detailed expense record of Direct Wages on a completed order; a Material Charges Sheet for production orders expense account; and a Direct Labor Summary.*

Factory Executive Service

13b.—Expense Analyses. Figure 20 illustrates a report that may be prepared by the Electric Accounting Machine either on a Daily, Weekly, or Periodical basis from the Distribution Cards which are punched for Indirect Wages and Material Expense. It is extremely important, particularly in plants wherein Indirect Labor and Material are budgeted that the foremen and factory operating heads be furnished with a Daily Analysis of the various items of Expense charged to each of the Operating Departments. In order to produce a report as illustrated in Figure 20, all Labor Tickets and Material Requisitions which have been punched for various expense charges are assorted daily by Department and Account classification. These cards are then tabulated and a statement produced for the benefit of the operating heads as illustrated.

13c.—Payroll Sheets. It is necessary to prepare for each pay period a report called a Payroll Register showing the name, social security number, clock number, hours worked, earnings, deductions, and net pay of each employee.

The Master card, the Gross Earnings card and the Deduction cards automatically compute and print this report on the Accounting Machine.

The same cards are then used to prepare automatically the payroll checks or payroll envelopes (used when payments are made in

Factory Cost Keeping

totals of Hours and Amounts are developed simultaneously as the Direct Wages Expense against each Part Number.

EXPENSE ANALYSIS

DEPT No	ACCT No	DESCRIPTION OF ACCOUNT	LABOR VALUE	MATERIAL VALUE
26	525	– Set-up	480	2250
26	529	– Supervision	310	390
			790*	2640*
27	525		450	430
27	528	– Accountant	78	50
27	530	– Timekeeper	45	200
27	531	– Secretary	835	895
27	532	– Clerk		80
27	635	– Stenographer		1460
			1408*	3115*
29	635		*	1280
				1280*
30	525		456	230
30	635			570
			456*	800*
31	526	– Bookkeeper		200
31	529	– Auditor	90	500
			90*	700*
32	526		138	
32	529		1050	8950
			1188*	8950*
33	528		200	110
33	530		310	450
			510*	560*
34	530		320	2000
34	532		1424	2980
			1744*	4980*
35	635		*	1090
				1090*
36	526		342	200
36	528		470	370
36	531		496	700
36	533	– Screw Machine	1156	17625
			2464*	18895*
37	525		114	
37	528		336	125
37	531		232	300
			682*	425*
38	528		54	60
38	530		135	
38	531		232	450
38	635			110
			421*	620*
39	635		*	368
				368*
40	530		195	240
40	635			115
			195*	355*

FIGURE 20. *Illustrating an analysis of Indirect Wages and Material Expenses by Department and Account Number.*

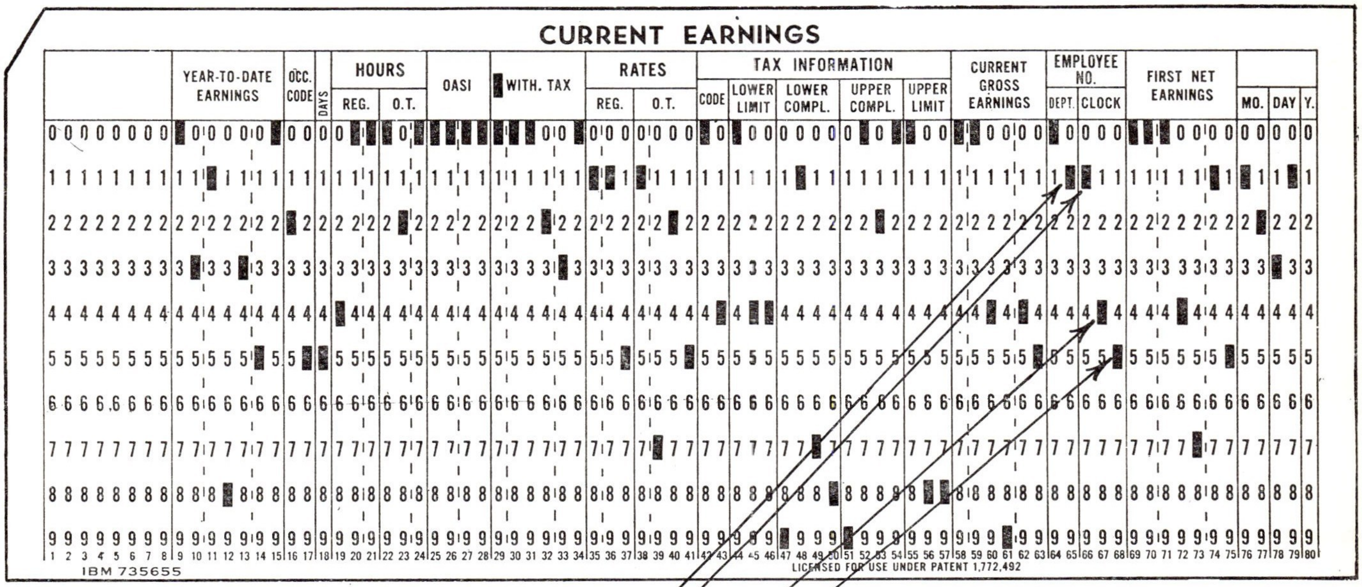

Gross Earnings Card

SHEET 1 OF 18

GENERAL MANUFACTURING COMPANY

PAYROLL REGISTER

DATE December 31

NAME / DESCRIPTION	EMPL. No. DEPT.	EMPL. No. CLOCK	TAX CODE	DAYS	BASE RATE	HOURS REGULAR	HOURS OVERTIME	CURRENT GROSS EARNINGS	DEDUCTIONS O. A. S. I.	DEDUCTIONS WITH. TAX	DEDUCTIONS OTHER	CURRENT NET PAY	YEAR TO DATE EARNINGS	YEAR TO DATE O. A. S. I.	YEAR TO DATE WITH. TAX
FRED ACKERLY	1	13	3		115										
WELFARE FUND											50				
GROUP INS											75				
ADVANCE											500				
WAR BOND											209				
				5		400		4600	46	360	834	3360	296894	2973	46185*
MILTON CARGIN	1	100	3		80										
SAVINGS											50				
				5		400	20	3440	34	110	50	3246	191991	1922	23950*
GERALD DRISCOLL	1	145	4		115										
WELFARE FUND											50				
SAVINGS											50				
WAR BOND											1875				
				5		400	20	4945		230	1975	2740	318350	3000	42140*
JAMES DUHLMEIER	1	150	6		65										
SAVINGS											50				
				5		400	20	2795	28	50	50	2667	200882	2011	8550*
CLEMENT EDWARDS	1	170	6		80										
WAR BOND											625				
				5		400	20	3440	34	60	625	2721	85256	854	6082*
JOHN EGGLESTON	1	175	5		80										
WELFARE FUND											50				
SAVINGS											50				
				5		400	20	3440	34	60	100	3246	164437	1648	5410*
WILLIAM FRISBIE	1	220	6		75										
SAVINGS											48				
PAYOFF											1714				
				3		240		1800	18	20	1762		231393	2317	14720*
SOCRATES GLEZEN	1	230	6		87										
WELFARE FUND											50				
SAVINGS											50				
				5		400	20	3741	37	70	100	3534	67074	673	4306*

FIGURE 21. *This shows the Gross Earnings Card punched for Gerald Driscoll. The arrows show how the card information shows up on the Payroll Register. Try to locate other information such as Earnings, Rate of Pay, Tax Code, etc.*

Factory Cost Keeping

cash) and statements of earnings and deductions.

The Payroll Register Figure 21, is produced on the Electric Accounting Machine by assorting the cards to Employee Number. Deductions are tabulated from cards punched for this purpose in complement in order to produce the net pay total which appears in the right hand column. Where Daily Reporting Cards are used, this report is produced without the necessity of assorting the Daily Reporting Cards as they have been filed daily in Employee Number sequence. Where Job Tickets are used, duplicate cards are sometimes punched daily for payroll purposes in order that the preparation of the Payroll will not interfere with the tabulation of the various cost records. In either case, the Payroll is produced exactly as it appears in Figure 21. It is a matter of preference when such a report is prepared.

Timekeeping and Payroll

13d. The timekeeping department carries the responsibility for the accuracy of recording attendance time and the notation of the proper allocation of this time to work-in-process or expense accounts. The primary functions are limited to the preparation of essential documentary records of employees' time, and policing their preparation to insure the accuracy of subsequent accounting entries.

Factory Executive Service

Jurisdiction over time clerks and shop recording is generally vested in the chief accounting officer—not the production executives. Employing this principle prevents the foreman from coercing the shop clerks to make improper allocations of time, thus covering up departmental inefficiencies.

Payroll is the accumulation of earnings and assembling of these data with related records, such as deductions. This is the primary purpose of the payroll department. In the performance of this function it must establish a record-keeping routine which will:

1. Establish the accuracy of individual employee earnings.
2. Furnish periodic earnings summaries for payroll disbursements.
3. Prepare essential voucher distribution records concerning payroll expenditures.
4. Supervise the preparation of payroll checks or cash pay envelopes.
5. Compile deduction lists such as OAB, UI, union dues, community chest, savings, welfare, etc.
6. Prepare employees' deduction receipts and earnings records.
7. Record unclaimed wages.
8. Provide management with current facts concerning overtime, piecework and daywork earnings, budget comparisons, etc.
9. Maintaining employees' earnings records in accordance with state and federal laws and regulations.

Factory Cost Keeping

Three Plans of Cost Department Routine

14.—Plan No. 1, Job Card, (Figure 11).

(a) The Job Cards are turned in to the Cost Department daily where they are rated and extended. Extensions of Piece Work and Day Work earnings are re-checked to prove the accuracy of the first extending operation.

(b) The cards are then passed to the key punch operator who transcribes the written data into terms of punched holes in the fields on the cards provided for this purpose.

(c) An adding machine total is taken of the Hours and Amount by Departments and this is checked against a like tabulation from the punched holes. If they agree, the fact is established that the cards have been punched correctly.

(d) A control total is thus established for each department which is posted to a Control Summary.

(e) The Hours are checked with the "In" and "Out" clock record which determines the fact that the Distribution in the form of the Job Cards, agrees in terms of Hours with the Attendance Record.

(f) Without the necessity for any further detail of posting in the Cost Department, the punched cards are then available for Payroll and subsequent labor and cost distributions.

14a.—Plan No. 2, Period Job Card,[*] (Figure 12). This plan is identical with the above except

[*]Continuous Job Card.

Factory Executive Service

that with the majority of the cards remaining in the shop for the entire pay period, a peak load condition is enforced upon the Cost Department. By the Electric Accounting Machine Method this peak load condition is taken care of without much trouble. By manual methods, the condition is met by adding more clerks to the staff and working more hours. Even then it takes several days in a good-sized factory to get out the Payroll or take care of special reports. The advantage of the Electric Accounting Machine method in this instance is its speed and general facility in handling this peak load condition and its accuracy.

14b.—Plan No. 3, Daily Reporting Card, (Figure 13). (a) As indicated in Paragraph 6, this form provides for a written record of all jobs performed by a workman each day.

(b) In some instances the "In" and "Out" attendance time record is also made on this card; in other instances on a separate clock card. When the total time is computed for the attendance record, it is checked with the total time reported against the various items of distribution on the Daily Reporting Cards. The daily time card in Figure 13 shows how the attendance record time is imprinted by the Attendance Time Recorder on the front of the Daily Reporting Card.

(c) The Daily Reporting cards are then rated and extended, either in the Timekeeping or Cost Departments. A reference to this card

Factory Cost Keeping

will indicate that fields are provided for punching Department, Man No., Hours, Amount and Rate. These captions for the fields are to be found across the bottom at the right of the card. The holes which have been punched in these fields are from the written information on the card. This completes the preparation of the card for tabulating the payroll.

(d) A Transcript or Trailer Card, also called a Distribution Card, is then punched for each item of distribution. Usually this is done at the same time that the Daily Reporting Card is punched and the two types of cards are interspersed. Consequently, the payroll hours and distribution hours for each man can be balanced easily with the Electric Accounting Machine. In Figure 13, the lower card is the distribution card. It will be noted that the upper card is for Order Number 1672 and the lower card is for Order Number 1672. Lines have been directed from the various descriptive data to the fields in which this information has been reproduced in terms of punched holes. More than one line from the written information pertaining to the second job (Order Number 1672) performed by the workman, has been drawn in the illustration to the distribution card at the right, in order not to confuse the reader. It will be seen, however, that the figures and written information pertaining to Order Number 1672 as shown on the Daily Reporting Card have all

Factory Executive Service

been punched into the Distribution Card.

(e) It will be seen that the Hours and Amount punched into the Distribution Cards (Transcript) must agree in total with the Hours and Amount punched into the Payroll Cards (Daily Reporting Card). Thus is provided the daily audit between the Payroll and Distribution.

(f) A control total is established by departments which is posted to a Control Sheet to which all subsequent reports must balance. The Payroll cards are then established in a Payroll File by Employee Number.

(g) The Distribution Cards are then assorted by the electric sorting machine into two groups, namely — Direct and Indirect Wages.

(h) The Indirect Wages are then tabulated by departments by accounts and a daily statement may be presented to the various Operating Heads and Production Foremen. This report is invaluable where expense labor is budgeted and provides extremely useful data to these operating people — *before the information becomes history.*[*]

(i) The Direct Wages reporting cards are assorted to Job or Order Number and after being tabulated into a Control Total, are filed in an "In Process" inventory file of Open Orders.

(j) The total is posted to an "In Process" inventory control sheet as a charge to "In

[*] See Figure 13a.

Process." The cards will remain in this open file until the orders are closed, at which time they are pulled and posted as a credit to "In Process" Control. The cards pulled for each closed order are then tabulated for all cost data and detail such as Parts, Operation, etc., pertaining to the finished order.

(k) Cost Records of all kinds may be tabulated periodically or at the end of the month, for closing entries.

Advantages of Daily Reporting Plan

15. The Daily Reporting Plan (Plan No. 3) just described has many advantages among which are:

1—Reduces clerical effort in shop by confining all reporting of wages to a single form each day.

2—Collects all wages for a workman on one form for purpose of locating discrepancies.

3—Fewer cards to handle, making easier checking.

4—Permits establishing of Payroll File by Employee Number independent of Cost Records, which is readily available in the event of Payroll disputes, Pay-offs, etc.

5—Permits immediate tabulation of Payroll at close of pay period, independent of tabulation of Cost Records, the latter being prepared from the Transcript cards.

Factory Executive Service

6—Provides daily audit between Payroll and Costs.

7—Precludes possibility of interference of split pay periods at close of calendar month.

Time Saved in Using Tabulating Machines

16. To demonstrate the factor of time saving, which is illustrated in this paragraph, a time study was made of the operations necessary to produce a finished Cost Record. An Order Number was selected to be analyzed for all the Wages charged to this Order, as represented by 250 Job Tickets. These cards had been previously punched, so they were then assorted into Part Number by Operation sequence in the sorting machine. The cards were then placed in the accounting machine which produced the Cost Record illustrated in Figure 19. The entire procedure was accomplished in 20 minutes. When it is considered that 7 columns were posted simultaneously, it will be appreciated that 1,750 items were posted, distributed, and accumulated into final Cost Record totals at a speed of 87 items per minute. This process can be cut down to as low as 12 minutes if time to get the machine started is eliminated.

Comparison with Hand Sorting and Hand Posting

17. If the same cost exhibit were to be prepared by hand, sorting and posting from

Factory Cost Keeping

job cards having the same written information, it is estimated that it would require 60 minutes to complete the exhibit. This estimate is divided as follows:

	Time Required
Sorting 250 Job Cards in 6 groups by parts	10 minutes
Sorting each group of Parts into 35 groups of operations (average 7 Job Cards per group)	20 minutes
Tabulating Total Pieces—Hours and Amount for each operation on adding machine and hand posting	20 minutes
Tabulating Total Pieces—Hours and Amount for each part	7 minutes
Tabulating Total Pieces—Hours and Amount for complete Order	3 minutes
Total	60 minutes

There is always the possibility of errors occurring in such an exhibit prepared by hand and the necessity of re-checking to prove the totals. The student should also keep in mind that such a time study as this is not the true measure of the value of an electric accounting machine system. A real showing is not made by a few hundred cards but the advantages are multiplied when there are thousands to be handled each day.

Chapter Ten

PAYROLL AND LABOR ACCOUNTING

Definition and Objectives

1. Payroll and Labor Accounting is reporting to the employee, to governmental agencies, and to the owners of a business, the amount of money paid for services rendered the employer by the employee. It includes the recording of the time the employee worked, the computation of his earnings and taxes, and the deduction from earnings of taxes and other deductible items to establish the net pay.

The following are the objectives of the Payroll and Labor application:

> Establish source documents, such as attendance and job records, which can also be used for payroll, cost, and production records.
> Make available complete, timely, accurate, and legible source records.
> Balance attendance time with job time.
> Establish good accounting control over payroll expenditures.
> Verify the accuracy of rates and extensions.
> Summarize earnings to compute Withholding Taxes.
> Prepare the Payroll Register.
> Prepare individual pay checks or envelopes.
> Prepare earnings and deduction statements for each employee.
> Prepare Deduction Registers.
> Prepare Federal Social Security records, Withholding Tax and Annual Income Tax figures.
> Produce State Unemployment Insurance and statistical reports.
> **Produce cost accounting records.**

Factory Cost Keeping

When an individual is employed, a "notification of employment" is prepared for the purpose of providing interested departments with data needed to establish employment and personnel records.

A Master Payroll Card is prepared from the personnel card (notification of employment) to provide the data needed to process the payroll records.

The employee fills out and signs a W-4 Form (U. S. Treasury Department) which provides the employer with the information necessary to compute the Withholding Tax on the employee's earnings.

The employee also signs authorizations covering deductions to be made from earnings, such as War Bonds, insurance, charitable donations, etc.

There are two major types of Deductions which the employer must deduct from Gross Earnings to determine the employee's Net Pay:

    Compulsory Types are:
      Withholding Tax.
      Old Age and Survivors Insurance.
      State Unemployment Compensation Insurance.

    Optional types are:
      War Bond Purchases.
      Insurance.
      Contributions — Red Cross, Community Fund, etc.

Factory Executive Service

Tools.
Uniforms.
Lunch Tickets.
Advances.
Union dues.
Other purchases.

2. Attendance time is the time the employee spends at the plant each day. Attendance time is the basis upon which the employee's pay is figured, except when piece work or incentive plans are used. If incentive or piece work plans are used, the employee's pay is figured on the basis of production. It is frequently necessary, however, to calculate the employee's earnings on an hourly basis to determine whether or not the employee, at piece work rates, is earning the minimum hourly rate required by law.

Even though attendance time may not be needed as a basis of figuring earnings, it is necessary to record "in" and "out" time. Accurate and legible recording of the time the employees spend in the plant provides:

Legally acceptable evidence in connection with compensation cases.
A basis for checking and setting piece rates.
Factual data required by the Federal Wages and Hours Law.

"In" and "out" Time Recorders are recognized as the most accurate and efficient means of recording attendance time.

Factory Cost Keeping

3. Job time is the time which the employee spends on particular jobs, processes, operations, etc. Accurate and legible recording of job time is necessary to provide accurate cost records. One of the best means of recording job time is through the use of the Job Recorder, Figure 5.

The following forms may be used for recording and distributing job time:

> Individual job card.
> Continuous job card.
> Gang job card.
> Daily time card, and trailer card punched from daily time card.

When the employee is employed, he is assigned a clock number for identification and is issued an attendance clock card. The clock card may be either "daily" or "pay period." This card is used to determine (1) the time the employee works for the employer and (2) the amount earned.

Daily, or at the end of the pay period, the attendance time is figured and entered on the clock card, either by writing or by marking.

Labor Accounting

4. Labor accounting is the classifying and accumulating of labor costs by order numbers and department expense accounts. This phase of accounting reveals to management the labor cost of the finished products.

The manner in which costs are distributed varies according to the nature of the product. Most cost systems fall into one of two general classes:

Process Cost Systems—A company manufacturing a staple or standard product for a steady market usually operates under a process cost system. In this type of industry, the same products are being continually processed. Process cost systems are used in the manufacturing of such products as oil, chemicals, paper, flour and textiles.

Job Order Cost Systems—A company manufacturing a specialty that has to conform to individual specifications would be required to quote selling prices in advance of production and would maintain job order costs to determine the profit on each job and to use as a guide in quoting prices and establishing selling prices on future orders. Job order cost systems are used by such industries as machine shops, foundries, and machine tool manufacturers.

Under either the process cost system or the job cost system, there are two classes of labor cost to be distributed:

Direct or production labor—charges which can be applied directly to a specific product, job, process, or department.

Indirect or non-productive labor — charges which cannot be applied to a specific product, job process, or department, such as cleaning, sweeping, supervising, clerical, or maintenance costs. Indirect costs, as a group, are commonly called "burden," "overhead," or "manufacturing expense."

5. Standard labor cost affords a means of determining what the labor used in pro-

Factory Cost Keeping

ducing a commodity should be. This value is established by calculating the time it should take to perform an operation and the money evaluation of the labor skill required. This is set as a standard, and costs are figured on the standard only, or on both the standard and the actual. The difference between the standard cost and the actual cost is called the variance. Standards may be used in either the process system or the job cost system.

Accounting Machines, because of their flexibility, are successfully applied to the accumulation of labor cost on process or job cost systems, with or without standards.

The source records for payroll distribution, in most cases, are the job tickets which are initially used to prepare payroll records. They may be either individual job cards, daily time cards, continuous job cards, or gang job cards.

Distribution cards punched for each job are balanced with the payroll controls by departments. They are then listed by man number on a report which is generally called the Labor Distribution Register. This is used for reference and to balance to control totals.

The direct labor job tickets are sorted out and filed in the work-in-process cost file behind the heading cards showing the order number, product number or operation number, depending on the basis for determining costs.

FACTORY EXECUTIVE SERVICE

Periodically, or when an order is completed, the cards are removed from the file and used to prepare detailed cost statements.

SHEET 2 OF 3

GENERAL MANUFACTURING COMPANY

INDIRECT LABOR

CLASSIFIED BY ACCOUNTS AND DEPARTMENTS — December 31

ACCOUNT No.	ACCOUNT NAME	DEPT.	HOURS	AMOUNT
211	SUPERVISION			
211		1	640	88 00
211		2	640	88 96
211		3	640	102 40
211		4	640	99 20
211		12	640	91 20
211		14	640	105 60
211		16	640	97 60
211		23	640	92 80
211		26	640	91 20
211		28	640	88 00
211		40	320	54 40
211		41	320	48 00
211		43	320	41 60
211		45	240	37 20
			7600	1126 16*
212	SET UP			
212		1	640	73 60
212		2	320	40 00
212		3	640	83 20
212		4	640	99 20
212		12	320	40 00
212		14	320	43 20
212		16	320	40 00
			3200	419 20*
221	ACCOUNTANT			
221		40	320	54 40
			320	54 40*
222	TIMEKEEPER			
222		40	960	147 20
			960	147 20*
223	SECRETARY			
223		40	320	48 00
			320	48 00*
224	STENOGRAPHER			
224		40	320	52 80
			320	52 80*
225	CLERK			
225		40	640	91 20
			640	91 20*

FIGURE 21a. *An example of an Indirect Labor Report by accounts.*

The indirect labor job tickets are filed in the expense file by date and account number. At the end of the accounting period, they are removed from the file and used to prepare a report of indirect labor (Fig. 21a) by accounts.

[108]

CHAPTER ELEVEN

ADMINISTRATIVE AND SELLING EXPENSE

Relation between Manufacturing and Other Expenses

1. The previous chapters have discussed the many different kinds of factors which are found in Manufacturing Expense and have shown the importance of these factors. But there are other factors of expense which have to be considered in a complete study of the costs of an article from the time it enters a factory as raw material until it is sold to dealers, jobbers, or consumers, as the case may be. As we study further into the subject, we find there are three distinct divisions of the Total Expense of any product. These are: Administrative Expense, Manufacturing Expense, and Selling Expense. Each of these is distinctly separate but there is a certain relation between these expenses.

1a. A manufacturing organization must have administrative officers to look after the company's general transactions, and such general functions which do not wholly belong to any one of the other divisions. The president, vice-president, secretary and treasurer are officers whose duties are of a general relation to the business. In a small organization they may serve in other capacities, and then their salaries are properly prorated depending upon the work they may do. It is necessary to have such officers to take care of the general business transactions, such as financing, banking, etc., in order to establish the Manufacturing Division. Likewise after a product is completed and ready for distribution there must be a Sales Division to advertise and sell the product. The General Manager is of course concerned in the expense necessary to conduct the business as a whole. The Sales Manager is concerned in the expense necessary to sell the goods. The Factory Manager is concerned only in the expense necessary to operate the factory properly and process the material.

Proper Application of Expense

2. The distinction between Manufacturing Expense, Administrative Expense and Sales Expense makes it possible to apply the expense at different periods. The Manufacturing Expense takes place while the materials and product are being processed or fabricated in the factory. It applies up to the point when the product is ready for shipment. The total of all Materials, Direct and Indirect Wages and Manufacturing Expense gives what is properly termed: "Factory Cost." The

Administrative Expense is incurred both while the product is being manufactured and also being sold and financed. This expense is properly added to Manufacturing Expense and the combined amounts make up what is termed as "Cost to Manufacture." Administrative Expense should be added however as a separate item and distinguished from actual "Factory Cost." The apportionment of Administrative Expense to the product should be on the ratio of benefit or involvement. The Selling Expense is properly applied to the product during the period in which it is sold. This is sometimes known as "Cost to Distribute." This added to "Cost to Manufacture" gives Total Cost which becomes the basis for pricing the product or service.

"Cost to Manufacture"

3. The Factory Manager is most interested in the costs which are under his jurisdiction and control. The figures furnished the Factory Manager should show the actual Factory Cost. Supplementary to such figures might be shown the "Cost to Manufacture" where the Administrative Expenses have been apportioned to each item. Because the Administrative and Selling Expenses are beyond the Factory Manager's control they should be apportioned and added as separate expenses to the product only after the Factory Costs have been accurately determined.

3a. When the Factory Cost and Administrative Expenses are combined into "Cost to Manufacture" the result is an accurate figure for inventories of finished products and work in process. If a fire should destroy all or a part of the product (both finished and in process) fair claims for losses can be made upon the insurance company for all of the expenses involved in replacing the goods to the same condition that prevailed before the fire. If any other figure than full cost or true inventory value were used in adjusting an insurance claim, the amount would be unfair to either the insurance company or manufacturer. The figures which make up the "Cost to Manufacture" therefore become accurate information about the value of inventories in accordance with recognized accounting procedure as well as in harmony with the regulations of the Internal Revenue Department of the Federal Government.

Keep Factory Cost Separate

4. Management policies are constantly towards the reduction of costs and expenses in an effort to increase the margin of profit or to proportionately lower selling prices and hold the markets against competition. Reduction of expenses can take place within each major division of an organization and cost figures should be so segregated that they will reflect every reduction that is made. Every reduction in expenses that the Factory Manager succeeds in making should be credited to his division and likewise reduction in Administrative or Sales Expense should be credited to the respective department. It is obviously unfair to the factory organization if they find ways and means of reducing costs and yet receive no recognition because division costs are not separated. Each division head and his staff are encouraged when cost figures pertaining to their division are so accumulated that full credit is given for every reduction in costs that is made.

4a. As the Manufacturing Expense is distributed to the product, whether the factory is operating at maximum capacity or on a greatly reduced schedule, the amount of Manufacturing Expense will vary widely and Factory Cost per Unit of Product will likewise vary. As long as only these expenses which properly belong to manufacturing are charged to the Factory Manager's Division, the expenses of the division are entirely within his control and he will do all he can to keep his Indirect Expenses as near a normal ratio to Direct Expenses as possible. In some cases the Administrative Expense can not be reduced as readily as Manufacturing Expense and when these two are combined into "Cost to Manufacture," the cost per unit of product will be proportionately higher in slack seasons compared to seasons of great activity.

The Factory Manager can not be especially blamed for such fluctuations. However, a separate statement of the Factory Costs apart from those of the other division enable the Factory Manager to apply more intelligent means of control to keep his costs as low as possible.

"Cost to Distribute"

5. Selling Expenses are sometimes termed: "Cost to Distribute." In this classification is included not only the expenses incurred to find buyers and consumers, but all of the expenses of carrying the goods, handling them, shrinkage while in stock, interest on investment in stocks, and delivery into the hands of the customer. Selling Expenses include, of course, sales administration, salesmen's salaries and commissions, advertising, as well as all items expended to enhance the prestige or good will of the concern.

Charging Interest on Investment

6. In Paragraph 2, of the Chapter: *Indirect Expense,* reference was made to the Interest Charge as one of the possible items of Indirect Expense. There is a division of opinion among accountants as to where the Interest Charge should be brought in. Some claim it is proper to set up the Interest Charge on Investment as one of the items of Indirect Expense. Others claim with equal forcefulness that the Interest Charge is rightfully brought in under the heading of Administrative Expenses. The recommendation of cost accountants and industrial engineers is that Interest be included in the costs as an item of Indirect Expense for *comparative* and *statistical purposes*. On the other hand auditors who are interested in the preparation of financial statements showing the condition of a business, maintain that to show Interest as an item of cost, inflates inventory values and anticipates profits. It must be admitted that inventory values are larger and that there is an anticipation of profits by exactly the amount of interest charged to the cost of goods on hand. However, in setting up inventory values in financial statements, the amount of interest previously charged, can be deducted in order to arrive at true values.

Relation of Interest to "Profit and Loss"

7. Investors put their money into a manufacturing enterprise in the hope of making more money (profit) on their investment than they would get if they deposited their money in a bank. The profit that is added after "Cost to Manufacture," and "Cost to Distribute" are totaled, and the selling price is established takes the place of interest on bank deposits or funds otherwise invested. Unfortunately manufacturing enterprises do

not always realize sufficient profit to equal a fair rate of return on the investment so it cannot be said that interest on the investment must always be met. Suppose a charge of 6% interest is made on capital invested as an element of manufacturing cost and yet in the "Profit and Loss" account of the business a loss of 2% is shown. Such a statement is erroneous. Actually the business has earned 4% net on the investment.

Proper Charge of Interest

8. There are cases where it is particularly desirable to include Interest in the costs. These are: (1) Where materials have to be stored for long periods while a seasoning process is being completed, and (2) Where it is desired to show the effect of variations in the amount of capital used and the length of time it is so used. In the first case, the seasoned material has a higher value than when first purchased, and it is quite evident that the interest on the capital tied up during the seasoning forms a part of the expense of such material. If seasoned material were purchased, a higher price would have to be paid in which the seller had included Interest and perhaps other carrying charges. In the second case, there are some manufacturing processes which require the use of expensive equipment or take a long time to complete. Both of these conditions tie up capital for some time,

whereas other manufacturing processes require neither the expensive equipment nor so long a time. In order to get a true comparison of costs in such cases it is necessary to give some consideration to the Interest on the capital invested.

Chapter Twelve

ANALYZING EXISTING COST SYSTEM

Steps in Making Analysis

1. For purposes of determining the value of an existing Cost System, a Factory Manager, Superintendent, Foreman, or anyone else may wish to make an analysis of it. A good procedure is to analyze the Cost System, first, from the standpoint of results obtained. "Is the most valuable information to the Factory Manager, the Administrative Officers, and Sales Manager being obtained and furnished to them in usable form?" should be one of the first questions to consider. If the results are all they should be, then the next approach might be to make an outline diagram representing the general plan of the Cost System and its various functions. It would be helpful to ascertain if all the objects and requirements of a good Cost System as shown in Figure 1 are taken care of.

Methods in Use

2. Further investigation should bring to light the various methods used in the Cost System under consideration and if these methods are suitable for the particular factory.

Factory Cost Keeping

A study should be made of the methods employed to determine if they are the best for obtaining the Labor Expense, Material Expense and Indirect Expense, both correctly and in the easiest and quickest manner possible. Consideration should be given to the amount and expense of clerical labor in obtaining these figures. On the other hand, the control of the factory might be dependent on very detailed costs, and that the information be furnished promptly following completion of the work or at frequent intervals. Daily Costs may be desirable and these can be furnished at the present time, with a combination of the pneumatic tube systems for dispatching the cost data from shop to office and the punch card system used on the tabulating machines, at comparatively low clerical expense.

Frills in System

3. A further analysis of an existing Cost System can well be made to determine if there is any unnecessary work being done or if records are duplicated. The more simple that the system is and still furnish the desired information, of course, the better. If the forms and records are simple and direct but serve the purpose, the system may be considered to be all right. However, the present day demands for cost information are so many and

varied that it may not be possible to keep the system a simple one. It may be necessary to have a rather elaborate system in order to obtain all the information desired. The measure of the success of such a system is in the amount of detailed cost data which it furnishes and the control which it gives to the Factory Manager. Even with a complex system, every effort should be made to avoid frills in the system which add to its operating expense but do not increase its value to the factory executives.

Head of Department

4. The third step in making an analysis of an existing Cost System is to consider the man in charge of the department. The Factory Cost Accountant should have those qualifications and requirements which are set forth in Chapter 12: *Factory Cost Accountant*. Inquiry should be made as to how well the head of the department measures up to these qualifications and requirements and how well he fits in with the general organization. The Assistant to the Factory Cost Accountant or the understudy to the position, should be measured in much the same way to determine his probable capabilities to assume charge of the work at some future time.

Questions Answered by Analysis

5. After going through the three steps of studying the *results* obtained by an existing Factory Cost System, investigating the routine of the *system itself,* and checking the qualifications of the *head of the department,* the following questions may be answered intelligently by the one making such an analysis. On the other hand these same questions may well be used as a guide in making the analysis:

1. Is the clerical force properly organized and working to the best advantage?
2. Is any useless information being collected?
3. Are there any short cuts that can be made in the figuring or posting?
4. Can any machines be used to reduce labor and obtain more accuracy?
5. Are the proper checks provided for payroll and is the payroll periodically audited?
6. Are the daily production records, together with spoiled work, being compiled in a way to be readily available?
7. Is a proper record of repairs, supplies and shop tools being kept by departments so that they are correct and available?
8. Is a detailed report of the Indirect Labor by departments being properly kept?
9. Are the proper records being kept to show the relation between the amount sold and the amount produced?

Factory Executive Service

10. Can one get, monthly, the value of product in dollars, per dollar of payroll or per dollar of general factory expense?
11. Do the records show the present value of any piece of equipment?
12. Can one get the cost of last year's repairs to any piece of machinery?
13. Is a proper record of the waste material being kept?
14. Does it provide a means of comparing the efficiency of different machines and workmen?
15. Can one get monthly comparisons of departmental expenses?
16. Can one get the details of the general factory expenses without unnecessary work?
17. Can one separate Factory Overhead from General Overhead?

We feel that when a Cost System will stand this analysis, and grade up to a satisfactory score, it ought to be well adapted to the business and be of considerable use to the Factory Manager.

Chapter Thirteen

FACTORY COST ACCOUNTANT

Personal Qualifications

1. The man in charge of a Factory Cost System should have the qualification of being methodical in everything which he does. He should keep the routine work of the Cost Department up to date and all records in an orderly manner. He should be a natural leader as much as any other foreman or department head. The Factory Cost Accountant should be able to figure out the everyday complications as they arise and through his own personal example be able to get results from his clerical staff. If he is a forceful character his staff will follow his good example in carrying out the details of the Factory Cost System. Also when necessary, he can insist on certain routine and get a willing response from every member of his department.

Knowledge and Experience

2. The ideal Factory Cost Accountant has some intimate knowledge of manufacturing, perhaps having worked in the manufacturing departments before taking up the field of Cost Accounting. As a substitute for the practical factory experience, the Factory Cost Accountant may have made a study of the manufacturing operations of one or several

different industries. He should constantly observe and study the operations and processes of the particular factory in order to keep posted on the changes that are always being made. This intimate knowledge of the factory work enables him to more intelligently guide and direct the Factory Cost Keeping System. At some time in his career, the Factory Cost Accountant should have experience in doing cost work before he assumes charge of an existing system or attempts to inaugurate a system in a different factory. The broader and more extensive that his experience may have been, the better prepared he will be to handle the details of his position.

Personal Accuracy

3. The ability of the Factory Cost Accountant to figure accurately and to reason out difficult problems and apply good judgment should be beyond question. He should be a good penman and be able to make neat figures with considerable rapidity. He should take pride in his work, not only as to its appearance, but with a sincere desire of accomplishment, striving always to have it the best he can make it.

Tact and Displomacy

4. The Factory Cost Accountant must be able to cooperate with all other departments

FACTORY COST KEEPING

of the factory. He is dependent on the manufacturing departments for correct data to make his own work right and therefore it pays him to keep the employees of all departments in proper sympathy with the work of Factory Cost Keeping, if he is to get the information needed. The Factory Cost Accountant and his staff must be tactful and diplomatic with all those with whom they come in contact. This is necessary in order to avoid friction with the Cost Department and the rest of the factory when securing the necessary data on costs. The Factory Cost Accountant should always keep in mind that the results of the Factory Manager in his control of factory and also help the factory departments in securing the cost data and then using it to the best advantage. Friendly relations between the Administrative Officers of an organization and the Cost Department will always bring better results to both parties.

Value Measured by Results

5. The Factory Cost Accountant should always be mindful that his job is to serve the work of his department is a measure of his own efficiency. It is results that he is after and he may find it advantageous to ask for help and cooperation from many sources. He

Factory Executive Service

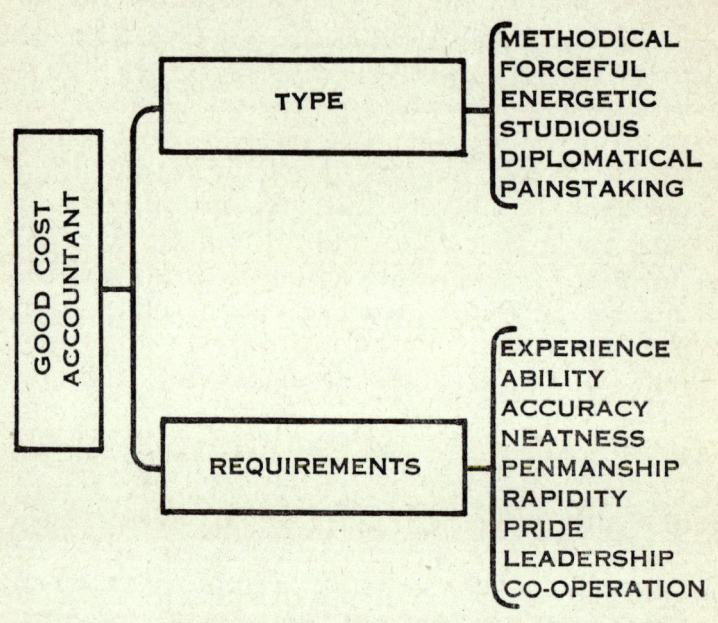

```
                    ┌─ METHODICAL
                    │  FORCEFUL
          ┌─ TYPE ──┤  ENERGETIC
          │         │  STUDIOUS
          │         │  DIPLOMATICAL
GOOD COST │         └─ PAINSTAKING
ACCOUNTANT┤
          │              ┌─ EXPERIENCE
          │              │  ABILITY
          │              │  ACCURACY
          │              │  NEATNESS
          └─ REQUIREMENTS┤  PENMANSHIP
                         │  RAPIDITY
                         │  PRIDE
                         │  LEADERSHIP
                         └─ CO-OPERATION
```

FIGURE 22. *Graphic Chart of Qualifications and Requirements of a Factory Cost Accountant.*

may have to make some personal sacrifices and extend his efforts along certain lines to obtain the desired results. The type of man suited for the work of Factory Cost Keeping and some of the requirements of the position are well presented graphically by Figure 22.

Chapter Fourteen

COST CONTROL AND THE FACTORY EXECUTIVE

Where Can Costs Be Controlled?

1. The principles of factory costkeeping which have been the subject of the previous chapters have dealt with the origin, incurring, calculation, and tabulations of costs. The prime purpose of having a cost system, however, is left to this final chapter. The principal purpose of maintaining a cost system is **cost control** and how such control can be exercised and achieved. To the student of factory management, the most important phase of cost control is the part played in cost control by the factory executive of today. Such is the gist of this chapter.

1a. Where the accounting department in the shop is concerned, it approches the job of controlling costs by analyzing reports and statements; by discovering pertinent facts about the costs of operation, and then analyzing these facts for whatever good they can get out of them that will benefit the whole shop. However, from the viewpoint of the "man in the shop", there are several very distinct instances where the **factory executive can exercise direct and effective control over costs.** The most important instances are: the work of the foreman; setting the rates; and the evaluation of each job.

What Kind Of A Man Does It Take?

2. The position of the factory executive on the foreman level cannot be under-estimated insofar as it affects cost control. Cost control really begins with the foreman, and the type of makeup he possesses determines how much cost control is exerted or overlooked on the production floor. The foreman who is able to exercise effective cost control must:

1. Know every detail of every operation under his supervision.
2. Be able to do each job as well if not better than the employee already on the job.
3. Be strict but fair, impartial and tactful toward his men.
4. Understand thoroughly every management policy he is given.
5. Have skill and technique in carrying out management's policies and decisions.
6. Be open-minded in his consideration of worker grievances.
7. Be fair in setting rates and job evaluation.
8. Know materials handling and materials flow.
9. Keep up the production pace without "cracking the whip".
10. Know plant layout for economy in machine and operations layout.
11. Be courageous enough to make decisions and stand by them.
12. Play no favorites in any instance.
13. Know his federal, state, dominion, province, or local labor laws—well.
14. Know his Labor-Management Contract in every detail.

Factory Cost Keeping

15. Know Quality Control and how to put it to work.
16. Be able to train his men with patience and skill.
17. Know the methods of payment of wages, deductions, bonuses, salaries, etc.
18. Be cost-conscious at all times.

Every single item in the list of "MUSTS" for cost control factory executives is pointed towards saving money by greater efficiency through controlling factory operations. It should be necessary to point to the last item as the most vital. Whatever help and facts or figures which the accounting office may give the factory executive, it will go for very little unless he is **fully cost-conscious**.

The Factory Executive's Cost Reports

3. Perhaps the most efficient way in which a factory executive is able to determine whether or not his department has been operating on an efficient and economic level, is by examining the cost report which refers to his own department. These reports are not and should not be considered so confidential (if confidential at all) that they should be seen only by top factory executives. A production level factory executive is the closest to costs and exercises first control; therefore, should be the first to examine these cost reports when issued by the cost department or accounting department. In all fairness to the first line factory executive it is one thing for top executives to **plan** better standards

FACTORY EXECUTIVE SERVICE

in order to lower costs, but quite another to achieve these standards on the shop floor. In most cases foremen would gladly cooperate if they were kept informed about cost facts as they concern their departments.

3a. The foremost cost report which should become a "must" for every foreman to examine carefully is the **"cost of production" report.**

	ELRAC CORPORATION MIDDLETOWN, USA			
WEEKLY COST OF PRODUCTION REPORT				
ITEM OF COST	(A) BUDGET	(B) ACTUAL	EXCESS	
			(A) over (B)	(B) over (A)
Direct Materials Direct Labor Overhead 1. Indirect Materials 2. Indirect Labor 3. Supplies 4. Tools 5. Maint. Materials 6. Maint. Labor 7. Power 8. Other				
Totals				
NET GAIN (Excess of (A) over (B)) NET LOSS (Excess of (B) over (A))				

FIGURE 23. *Sample Cost of Production Report.*

This form should show the **direct material costs, direct labor costs,** and **overhead costs** for each unit or department over a given period of time. The Figure 23 shows such a report.

Factory Cost Keeping

In some reports the quantities of each item produced is also shown. This allows a breakdown in costs per item. The foreman who is handed such a report cannot help but take the highest interest in its contents because they represent the results of his job, the work in his own department. He can take pride in a good report, or let it build up his determination to put in extra effort when the report is not satisfactory. Whatever the effect of his report, he remains secure in the fact that nothing is being withheld from him.

3b. In many plants, **defective work (scrap) reports** are handed to the foreman daily, or weekly. In other instances foremen are required to make up these reports themselves. Such a report shows an analysis of the costs incurred by poor work which fails to pass inspection. It also spurs a conscientious foreman to increase his supervision over quality control methods, if such are in use, and maintenance of quality standards so as to keep down the cost of scrap or work which may later require re-operation to bring it up to standard.

A **material and labor report** showing budget allowances is very often given to the factory executive on the foreman level. The budget allowances are shown in comparison with actual costs. If the standards have been set skillfully in the beginning, there is little variation which will occur in the costs. One item over which the foreman can exert direct control of costs

FACTORY EXECUTIVE SERVICE

is controllable overhead costs. He should be given frequent reports on this item so that he can exercise sounder management principles to keep this cost down. Dollar amounts and percentages should be shown on this report. As an added incentive (discussed later), a bonus plan may be effected to award the foreman a part of the saving in actual controllable overhead expenses below certain budget allowances designated at the time the allowances are determined. Such bonuses are long-time plans so that averages may be absorbed in favorable economic periods. Payment of such bonuses are semi-annual or annual.

3c. **Idle machine reports** and **idle labor reports** are of high concern to the foreman. It is his responsibility to determine whether the cause for high costs be lack of material, faulty planning, or poor maintenance, and then do something constructive about it. **Repair costs reports** are also indicators of cost control centers. These should be set up to compare the present period (week, month) with preceding periods as well as show the repair costs for an average month. Where a standard cost system is in use, the foreman should be furnished with an analysis showing the variation of his department's cost as compared to other similar departments, or periods of time, or both.

From time to time such miscellaneous reports and statements should be supplied to the factory executive as are dictated by present circumstances. The main point to bear in mind is that these reports be kept as uniform and understandable (brief, clear and simple) as is possible. Quite often the use of bar, circle or line graphs is a boon towards understanding the report. It should also go without saying that too many reports can often become an avalanche of "paper work" which defeats the very purpose for which reports are set up.

Making Cost Control Worthwhile To The Factory Executive

4. Since the production line factory executive is the most important single item in controlling costs, it is logical that an effective incentive bonus for the foreman would be a positive step. The foreman's wage has always been a subject for discussion. However, to add to this wage, a bonus payment for costs which are reduced is undeniably effective. In setting up such a bonus plan, several vitally important guideposts must be kept in mind. These factors are:

1. Cooperation with other factory executives and workers.
2. Effective results in training new workers.
3. Number and occurence of accidents.
4. The ratio (also percentage) of his unit or section's labor costs to total departmental labor costs.
5. Effectiveness in meeting quality and quantity standards.
6. Credit points for attendance, turnover, idle time, scrap reduction, inspection ratings, unit costs.

Factory Executive Service

4a. While these factors are general, they point the way to an incentive bonus plan which will effectively encourage foremen to control and reduce costs. Quantity of work is vital, but quality is not second to quantity. Quite often, the stress on quantity brings about vicious cutthroat competition rather than cooperation between departments. The factors above such as quantity, quality, costs, and turnover are tangible and measurable. However, intangible factors such as cooperation and enthusiasm are not measurable, therefore must be rated. Tangible and intangible factors to be used in the same instance render it hard to design an analysis sheet of the foreman's job. This means that an incentive bonus plan is by the same token, difficult to devise. Consequently, the job of setting up a fair bonus system to encourage foremen to control costs more closely needs much forethought and the tangible (measurable) factors should be given the greater weight (about 75%) in the analysis sheet. The intangibles (rated factors) should be present to about 25% of the necessary weight given to all the factors on the analysis sheet.

4b. A sample bonus plan might consist of these three factors: (1) cost reduction, (2) output, and (3) a point by point award for improving the rating on intangible factors. In such a plan, two of the factors are tangible while the third is intangible or immeasurable except by rating. Cost reduction can be measured in many ways depending on the ingenuity of the bonus plan maker. Output is measurable and ought to be judged against both quantity and quality standards, plus a consideration of related factors, (scrap, waste, etc.).

In almost all instances the production factory executive's bonus for controlling costs should be expressed as a per cent of his base wage or pay. With such an incentive to which to look forward, the factory executive has a basic human reason to urge him to more effective cost control.

BIBLIOGRAPHY

ALFORD, L. P., "Management's Handbook," The Ronald Press, New York, 1924.

ALFORD, L. P., BANGS, J. R., "Production Handbook," The Ronald Press, New York, 1944.

BETHEL, L. L., et al, "Industrial Organization and Management," McGraw-Hill Book Co., Inc., New York, 1945.

CARROLL, P., Jr., "Time Study for Cost Control," McGraw-Hill Book Co., Inc., New York, N. Y.

CHARTER, H. G., "Standard Costs, "The Ronald Press, New York, 1930.

DRESSEL, W. D., "How Proper Cost Information Can Increase Profits," N. A. C. A. Bulletin, Vol. 27, No. 2, September 15, 1945.

DINGMAN, C. F., "Estimating Building Costs," McGraw-Hill Book Co., Inc., New York, N. Y.

HENRICI, S. B., "Standard Costs for Manufacturing," McGraw-Hill Book Co., Inc., New York, N. Y.

NORDHOFF, W. A., "Machine-Shop Estimating," McGraw-Hill Book Co., Inc., New York, N. Y.

PATTERSON, T. H., "Standard Costs as an Aid to Management," N. A. C. A. Bulletin, Vol. 26, No. 15, April 1, 1945.

RALSTON, A. W., "Budgetary Control," Lincoln Extension Institute, Inc., Cleveland, Ohio, 1951.

SPECTHRIE, S. W., "Industrial Accounting," Prentice-Hall, Inc., New York, 1946.

TORNBORGH, B. V., "Talking Costs," Supervision Magazine, Volume V, No. 5, May, 1943, page 12. (Continued in each issue of Supervision Magazine through December, 1943).

TORNBORGH, B. V., "The ABC of Shop Costs," Supervision Publishing Company, 95 Madison Ave., New York 16, N. Y.

INDEX

INDEX

Account, Scrap, 25-26
    material, 25-26
Accountants' Association, 1
Accounting, payroll and labor, 102
Analysis of existing cost system, 118
    methods in use, 119
    frills, 119-120
    questions answered by, 121-122
Attendance Record Card, weekly, 59-60
Attendance Recorders, 59, 63
Attendance time, defined, 104
Automatic time recorder, 61

Business, danger of, without cost system, 8
    danger to, by absence of, 8
Budget, allowances, 131

Cards, Daily Time, 4
    job cost, 66
    examples job cost, 67
    daily reporting, 74
    trailer, 76
Continuous Job Card, 73
Continuous Production System, 51-52
Contribution deductions, 103
Control of Time, 58
Cost Accountant, 123
    personal qualifications, 123-125
    value of results by, 125-126
Cost Accounting, relation of time, 54
Cost Control, 127
    purpose of, 127
    by factory executive, 127, 128-129
Cost Department, 9
    purpose of cost system in, 9-10, 11
    work of, 10-11
Cost Department Routine, three plans of, 95-96, 97-98, 99
Cost distribution, 106
    classes of labor distributed, 106
Cost factors, 16
Cost of Manufacturing, fundamental elements, 16
Cost Records, 53
    need for accurate, original, 53
Cost Report, 129
    and factory executive, **129**
    types of, 130
    production, 130
Cost Sheet, example, 23
    defined, 24
Cost System, 1, 3, 5
    three reasons for, 5-6, 7
    and Factory Manager, 6
    importance to factory manager, 7
    how it helps factory, 8
    and Cost Department, 9-10, 11
    objects of, 13
    requirements of, 14
    plan, 31
    indirect expense, 32
    process, 106
    job order, 106
    steps in making analysis, 118
Costs, historical, 3
    controllable overhead, 132
    daily, 4
    standard, 4
    standard, fundamentals, 4
    determined, 4
    determining production, 5-6
    distributing direct labor, 10-11
    distributing material, 10-11
    control by foreman, 128-129
    calculation other costs in fabricating, 11
    practical limits of accuracy, 15
    indirect expense, 15
    depend upon accurate time records, 53
    collecting with machines, 71
    overhead, report, 130

Daily Costs, 4
Daily Reporting Plan, advantages, 99-100
Daily Reporting Time Card, 62, 74
Daily Time Cards, 4
    In-Process Inventory, 4
Daily Time Ticket (Card), 75
Deductions, payroll, 103-104
    defective work, reports, 131
Departmental expenses, 26, 50
    applying, 51
Depreciation expense, 34
    determining rate of, 34-35, 36
Determined Costs, 4
Direct Labor, 27, 106, 130
    Cost Analysis, 77
    defined, 106
Direct Labor Costs, distributing, 10-11
Direct Material Cost Report, 130
Distribution, cost of, 114

Electric Card Punching Machine, 80
Electric End Printing Reproducing Punch, 79
Electric Punched Card Accounting Machine, 83-84
    value of, 86
Electric Punched Card Accounting Machine Method, 71
    scope of use, 87-88, 89-90
    reports developed by, 90-91
    time saved in use of, 100
Electric Punched Card Sorting Machine, 81-82
Electric Punched Hole Verifier, 81
Expense analyses, 92
Expenses, indirect, 15, 32
    material, 21
    determining, 21
    departmental, 26, 50
    labor, 27
    depreciation, 34
    variable, 36-37
    factory, 38-39
    Total, 109
    administrative, 109
    selling, 109
    proper application of, 110
    manufacturing, 109

INDEX

cost to manufacturer, 111
cost to distribute, 114

Factory Cost Keeping, 1-2
Purpose of, 1
limitations of, 2
old method, 3
Factory Cost System, 9
graphic outline of typical, 12
Factory Expenses, 38-39
calculation of, 39-40
inaccuracy of calculations, 40-41
Factory Manager, 3
importance of cost system to, 7
use of cost system to, 7-8
Federal Income Tax, 1
Fixed Charges, 33-34
items in, 33
Foreman, **cost controls, 128-129**

General Accounting, relation of cost system to, 5

Heat, 37
Historical Costs, 3

Idle Machine, **reports, 132**
labor **reports, 132**
Indirect Expense, 15, 32
accuracy in distributing, 15
first indication of, 17-18
main items, 19
factors of, 33
percentage plan, 39-40
productive hour plan, 41-42
machine hour method, 43-44
Indirect Labor, 27-28, 106
defined, 106
example of report, 108
Indirect Wages, 31
Insurance deductions, 103
Interest, relation to profit **and loss,** 115
proper charge of, 116
charging, on investment, 114
Investment, charging interest on, 114

Job Card, 72
Continuous, 73
Job Cost Cards, 66
information on, 67
examples of, 67
Job Cost Recorders, 68
examples, 68
use of, 69
Job Time, 57
defined, 105
forms for recording, 105

Labor, 27
defined, 27
indirect, 27-28, 106
importance of correct records, 27
expenses, 27
accounting, 105
costs report, 130

Labor Expenses, 27
importance of correct records, 27
Light, 37

Machine Hour Method, 43-44
Machine hours, value of, 46
Manufacturers' Association, 1
Manufacturing costs, three fundamentals, 15
examples, 17-18
complications in, 18-19
Manufacturing expenses, 119
relation to other expenses, 109
Master Time and Program Control, 64
Material, direct, 21
costs report, 130
indirect, 21
and labor, report, 131
which is cut up, 24
Material Account, 25-26
Material Costs, distributing, 10-11
Material expenses, 21
determining, 21
Mixed Labor, 29
Modern Time Stamps, 65

Old Age and Survivors Insurance, 103

Payroll, 93
sheets, 92-93
defined, 94
distribution source records, 107
Payroll and labor accounting, 102
defined, 102
objectives, 102-103
deductions, 103-104
Payroll Dial Recorder, 63
Payroll Time, 57
Percentage Plan, 39
Power, 37
Production costs, determining, 5-6
Production Report, Costs, 130
Productive Hour Plan, 41
complications of, 43

Recorder, Payroll Dial, 63
attendance time, 63
Repairs, 37

Scrap Account, 25-26
Standard Costs, defined, 4
basis for, 4
derived from, 4
makeup of, 4
fundamentals, 4,
State Unemployment Compensation Insurance, 103

Ticket, Daily Time (Card), 75
gang job, 76-77
Time, recognition, value of, 53
relation to cost accounting, 54
control, 54-55
records of, in wage payment methods, 56-57
payroll, 57
job, 57

[142]

INDEX

control, 58
  automatic recorder, 61
  daily reporting card, 62
  master program control, 64
  modern stamps, 65
Timekeeping, 92-93
Trailer Card, 76
  transcript, 97
  distribution card, 97

Variable expenses, 36-37

War Bond Purchases, 103
Withholding Tax, 103
Work, defective, reports, 131
Workmen, not trained
  accountants, 55
Workmen's Compensation
  Insurance, 37